RANDALL JARRELL

SELECTED POEMS

THE WOMAN AT
THE WASHINGTON ZOO

RANDALL JARRELL

SELECTED POEMS

INCLUDING

THE WOMAN AT
THE WASHINGTON ZOO

NEW YORK ATHENEUM *1974*

Published in Canada by McClelland & Stewart, Ltd.
Manufactured in the United States of America by
The Murray Printing Company
Forge Village, Massachusetts
First Atheneum Edition August 1964
Second Printing October 1966
Third Printing September 1968
Fourth Printing October 1969
Fifth Printing March 1974

SELECTED

POEMS

RANDALL

JARRELL

TO

Mary,

Alleyne,

AND

Beatrice

INTRODUCTION

In THIS *SELECTED POEMS* THERE ARE TEN poems from my first book, some of them a great deal changed; almost all the other poems come from *Losses*, *The Seven-League Crutches*, or *Little Friend, Little Friend*. I left out "Orestes at Tauris" because, though I like it and some readers like it, it's very long, it's an earlier poem than any of these, and it's back in print in the new edition of *Losses*. I left out several poems that I am still working on. Only two poems, "A War" and "The Survivor Among Graves," are new; they belong with other poems about the war, and not with the poems I have written in the last three or four years.

I have read these poems many times to audiences of different sorts, and all the audiences liked listening to them better, and found them easier, if I said beforehand something about what a ball turret was, or a B-24, or Tatyana Larina—and said it in "plain American that cats and dogs can read." Not that my poems aren't in plain American, but there it's verse, not prose. Prose helps; it helps just by being prose. In the old days, when readers could take or leave prose, poets sometimes gave them a good deal of it: there are hundreds of pages of notes and prefaces and reminiscences in Wordsworth's or Tennyson's *Collected Poems*. But nowadays, unless you're reading Marianne Moore or Empson or *The Waste Land*, you rarely get any prose to go along with the poems.

The war—the Second World War—has been over for a long time; there are names and events people knew they would never forget which, by now, they have forgotten they ever knew. Some of these poems depend upon, or are helped by, the reader's remembering such names and events; other poems are helped by the reader's being reminded of some particular story or happening or expression—something you remember if you have lived in the South, or been in the Air Force, or gone to *Der Rosenkavalier*, or memorized some verse of the Bible. I've put into this introduction some prose sentences about a few of these things. But they are here for the reader only if he wants them—if you like poems without prose, or see after a few sentences that I am telling you very familiar things, just turn past this introduction.

A Girl in a Library is a poem about the New World and the Old: about a girl, a student of Home Economics and Physical Education, who has fallen asleep in the library of a Southern college; about a woman who looks out of one book, Pushkin's *Eugen Onegin*, at this girl asleep among so many; and about the *I* of the poem, a man somewhere between the two. A *blind date* is an unknown someone you accompany to something; if he promises to come for you and doesn't, he has *stood you up*. The Corn King and the Spring Queen went by many names; in the beginning they were the man and woman who, after ruling for a time, were torn to pieces and scattered over the fields in order that the grain might grow.

Some of my readers will say with a smile, "And now aren't you going to tell us who said, 'Against stupidity the gods themselves struggle in vain'? who said, 'Man wouldn't be the best thing in this world if he were not too good for it'? who had said to him, as a boy, 'Don't cry, little peasant'?" No. This would take too much space, and would be a sort of interference with the reader—and I don't want to do any more, in this introduction, than put in an occasional piece of information that may be useful to some readers.

THE KNIGHT, DEATH, AND THE DEVIL is a description of Dürer's engraving, and the reader might enjoy comparing the details of the poem with those of the picture.

In *Der Rosenkavalier* the Marschallin, looking into her mirror, says that yesterday everybody called her *little Reti*, and tomorrow everybody will be calling her *the old woman, the old Marschallin*. I used her words as an epigraph for THE FACE.

LADY BATES is a little Negro girl whose Christian name is *Lady*. Mock oranges are also called Osage oranges—they look like giant green navel oranges, and are impressive to children. *Trifling* means *worthless, good-for-nothing, no-account*, and is often used affectionately. In the South convicts used sometimes to be farmed out as servants.

When Heine met Goethe he told him that he was working on "my *Faust*," and Goethe grew very cold. This CONVERSATION WITH THE DEVIL isn't anybody's *Faust*, but it does have many allusions to the Devil's past, and a good many to our own past and present. Fortunately, one can understand the poem without recognizing any of the allusions. Let me mention three, though: Will Rogers' "I never saw the man I didn't like"; the old lady who had found so much comfort in repeating "that blessed word, Mesopotamia"; and the little boy in Hardy who wrote, "We was too many."

Seele im Raum is the title of one of Rilke's poems; "Soul in Space" sounded so glib that I couldn't use it instead. An eland is the largest sort of African antelope—the males are as big as a horse, and you often see people gazing at them, at the zoo, in uneasy wonder.

The Night Before the Night Before Christmas takes place in the year 1934; the girl is fourteen. The part about the "cotton-wool that is falling from the ears of God" is a Scandinavian joke that has become a family joke in the little family of the girl and her brother. *The Iron Heel* is a book by Jack London about the workers' fight against the Fascist state of the future. *The Coming Struggle for Power* is a book, once well known, by John Strachey. The girl's father is a Lion, a Moose, just as he might be an Elk or Rotarian or Kiwanian. "In Praise of Learning" is a song, very firm and haunting, with words by Bert Brecht and music by Hans Eisler; in those days it ran through many heads besides the girl's. Both Engels and Marx are real and present figures to the girl, who has got as far, in *Capital*, as the chapter on the working day, and is reading it that night. She has read *A Tale of Two Cities* at school, and Sidney Carton's "It is a far, far better thing I do . . . ." is there in her mind along with Martha and Mary, her squirrel, her brother, and all the other people less fortunate than she.

The Black Swan is said, long ago, by a girl whose sister is buried under the white stones of the green churchyard.

There is a quilt-pattern called The Tree of Life. The little boy, sick in bed, has a dream in which *good me* and *bad me* (along with the uncontrollable unexplainable *the Other*) take the place of Hänsel and Gretel.

In IN THE WARD: THE SACRED WOOD, the wounded man has cut trees from paper, and made for himself a sacred wood; with these, the bed-clothes, the nurse, the doctor, he works his own way through the Garden of Eden, the dove and its olive-leaf, the years in the wilderness, the burning bush, the wars of God and the rebel angels, the birth and death and resurrection of Christ.

I put into A GAME AT SALZBURG a little game that Germans and Austrians play with very young children. The child says to the grown-up, *Here I am*, and the grown-up answers, *There you are;* the children use the same little rising tune, and the grown-ups the same resolving, conclusive one. It seemed to me that if there could be a conversation between the world and God, this would be it.

AN ENGLISH GARDEN IN AUSTRIA is a poem about neo-classicism changing into romanticism, the eighteenth century changing into the nineteenth. Someone going home from an Austrian performance of *Der Rosenkavalier* thinks the poem—thinks it when he comes across an English garden, the first outpost of romanticism there on the Continent. He thinks of Madame de Maintenon's *Athalie* replaced overnight by Nature, with all its ruins and prospects; thinks of Baron Ochs von Lerchenau meeting Rousseau and oldfashionedly mistaking him for Metastasio; and then thinks of the greatest singer of Metastasio's operas, the castrato Farinelli—of Farinelli's life in Spain and in the Italy of the Arcadian Academy, that Academy which lasted long enough to have Goethe for a member. The man, looking at the false ruin inside the garden, the real ruins outside it, thinks of the days when Voltaire ruled Europe, and Frederick the Great could call *Götz von Berlichingen* "a play worthy of the savages of Canada"; thinks of some of the things that led up to, or accompanied, the French Revolution; and thinks at length of that Napoleon Bonaparte who seems to him a precursor of our own time, of the petty bourgeois water-colorist Hitler, of the spoil-sport from a Georgian seminary, Stalin. The present speaks to him in Marx's "Others have understood the world; we change it"; in the pragmatists' "Truth is what works"; in Lincoln Steffens' statement about Russia, "I have seen the Future and it works." Some voices from the opera he has just seen reply, in wondering and helpless opposition, and end with the Marschallin's *Today or tomorrow comes the day—* her *And how shall we bear it? Lightly, lightly.* For a moment the city and its ruins seem to the man the city of the earth, dead, and troubled by a ghostly air.

I can hear the reader's despairing, "Oh, *no!*" so clearly that I hate to tell him that a certain amount of A RHAPSODY ON IRISH THEMES is a sort of parody of the *Odyssey*. In the original it's not an adding-machine but an oar that no one must be able to recognize; and I am able to call Ireland *you enclave of Brünn and of Borreby man* only because of reading (and, better still, looking at the pictures in) Carleton Coon's *The Races of Europe*.

The hero of SEARS ROEBUCK, clad, housed, and supplied with a pronouncing Bible by the great mail-order firm, is frightened by other portions of its catalogue, and sees before him the fire of judgment.

The hero of MONEY, an old man surviving into a different age, says the poem during the '20's, when businessmen used to say that they worked not for money but for

Service. *Miss Tarbell* is Ida Tarbell, the famous muckraker; *Ward* is Ward MacAlister, equally famous as a "social arbiter." The city of Providence is the capital of Rhode Island. The old man's *But giving does as well* means that when you have bought everything there is to buy, you have only begun: you can still establish foundations, make bequests with conditions, and say *Go* and *Come* in many tax-exempt ways—money, in this "aetherealized" form, is as powerful as ever.

Galileo, Newton, and Bruno are the great emancipators addressed in the first stanza of The Emancipators.

La Belle au Bois Dormant is a poem about a murdered woman; her body has been put in a trunk, and the trunk checked in a railway station.

Eighth Air Force is a poem about the air force which bombed the Continent from England. The man who lies counting missions has one to go before being sent home. The phrases from the Gospels compare such criminals and scapegoats as these with that earlier criminal and scapegoat about whom the Gospels were written.

A ball turret was a plexiglass sphere set into the belly of a B-17 or B-24, and inhabited by two .50 caliber machine-guns and one man, a short small man. When this gunner tracked with his machine-guns a fighter attacking his bomber from below, he revolved with the turret; hunched upside-down in his little sphere, he looked like the foetus in the womb. The fighters which attacked him were armed with cannon firing explosive shells. The hose was a steam hose.

At one time in the Second Air Force—the bomber training command—one member of every bomber crew was ordered to learn to play the ocarina "in order to improve the morale of the crews overseas." It was strange to walk along a dark road and look up at the big desert stars and hear from the distant barracks a gunner playing his ocarina. The hero of TRANSIENT BARRACKS, after some years abroad as a gunner, is a gunnery instructor now. A *G.I. can* is what you and I would call a garbage can; a *'24* is a B-24, a Liberator, a bomber very like a truck. In a *day-room* soldiers spend their evenings shooting pool, or listening to the radio, or writing home. When you shaved in barracks you usually had the choice of a broken glass mirror in which you could recognize part of yourself, or a mirror of unbroken metal in which you could see a face. The *C.Q.* is the soldier in Charge of Quarters. Before a man left a field every department of the field had to sign a clearance saying that he had kept nothing of theirs—but as you see, everyone went away with something.

SIEGFRIED is a poem about a gunner in one of the B-29's which bombed Japan. *To enter so many knots in a window, so many feet:* to enter speed and altitude in a gunsight or bombsight.

In A PILOT FROM THE CARRIER, *genius* is another form of the word *jinnee.*

The title, PILOTS, MAN YOUR PLANES, is the command repeated over the communication system of the carrier; the sound which accompanies it is like the sound of a *giant's jew's-harp. The steel watch-like fish:* torpedoes were called *fish. But on the tubes the raiders oscillate:* on the tubes of the radar sets. *A mile in every nine or thirteen seconds:* nine if they were the fighters, thirteen if they were the torpedo-planes. *Great light buckles . . . raft's hot-water-bottle weight:* the pilot's parachute and rubber life-raft are strapped to him, and dangle at his back. *Locked at last into the bubble,*

Hope: the cockpit of the plane has a molded tear-drop canopy. *His gear falls:* his plane's retracted landing-gear falls when he flies into the fire from his own carrier.

THE DEAD WINGMAN: a fighter pilot, on a carrier off Japan, keeps searching in his sleep for his shot-down wingman.

STALAG LUFT: a (German) Prison Camp for Air Force Enlisted Men. One of the American prisoners is speaking.

JEWS AT HAIFA: in the first year and a half after the war ended, many of the Jewish survivors who had left Europe for Palestine were sent from Haifa to concentration camps on the island of Cyprus.

The men in PRISONERS are American prisoners of Americans. They wear a white *P* on their dark blue fatigue clothes. Before and during the first years of the war, this *P* was, instead, a white ball like the bull's-eye of a target: it was there for the M.P. to shoot at if the prisoner tried to escape.

The men in O MY NAME IT IS SAM HALL are three American prisoners and one American M.P., at a B-29 training base in southern Arizona. The guard's song begins
O my name it is Sam Hall, it is Sam Hall.
O my name it is Sam Hall, it is Sam Hall.
O my name it is Sam Hall
And I hate you one and all—
Yes, I hate you one and all,
God damn your eyes.

A CAMP IN THE PRUSSIAN FOREST: An American soldier is speaking after the capture of one of the German death camps. Jews, under the Nazis, were made to wear a yellow star. The Star of David is set over Jewish graves as the Cross is set over Christian graves.

Out of the desert of southern Arizona—a desert spotted with training fields for bombers and fighters—isolated mountain ranges rise nine or ten thousand feet, like islands from a sea of sand. LEAVE is said by a man who is spending a furlough on one of these.

In A FRONT, a front is closing in over a bomber base; the bombers, guided in by signals from the five towers of the radio range, are landing. Only one lands before the base is closed; the rest fly south to fields that are still open. One plane's radio has gone bad—it still transmits, but doesn't receive—and this plane tries to land and crashes.

In SECOND AIR FORCE the woman visiting her son remembers what she has read on the front page of her newspaper the week before, a conversation between a bomber, in flames over Germany, and one of the fighters protecting it: "Then I heard the bomber call me in: 'Little Friend, Little Friend, I got two engines on fire. Can you see me, Little Friend?' I said, 'I'm crossing right over you. Let's go home.' "

In THE RISING SUN, the word *fault* is used in its geological sense. *A five-colored cloud:* an emperor once ordered a year's celebration because a five-colored cloud had been observed by a provincial official. *From its six-cornered roof upon the world:* the roof of the Japanese world, like the roof of a Japanese house, has six corners. *Heads roll/ From the gutted, kneeling sons by rule:* in hara-kiri the kneeling man slashes his abdomen, and his head is cut off by his attendant. *The warrior/ Who bowed in blue, a child of four:* schoolboys were given blue uniforms at that age. *The child's grey ashes . . . the shrine beside the rocks . . . a lacquered box*

. . . *and take the last dry puff of smoke:* the soldier's ashes were shipped home and placed in a temple by his mother or wife, who lit a cigarette for him and took a last puff of smoke in his memory. Motion pictures of this ceremony were shown to our army as part of a documentary film on Japan.

New Georgia: this is an island in the South Pacific. Americans captured it; the speaker is one of them, a Negro.

The Subway from New Britain to the Bronx: this poem's "sparrow" lived among the orchids of subway advertisements and died among the orchids of the rain-forests of the island of New Britain. He came there from the Bronx, where as a child he wandered through the largest zoo in the world, mocking the animals behind its bars.

A Ward in the States: these soldiers are malaria patients home from the South Pacific, in Army hospitals.

The Dead in Melanesia: *Melanesia* means *the black islands.* The *trades* are the trade winds. In parts of Melanesia the most important sacred object is the nautilus-like spiral which a boar's tusk forms when the tusk in the jaw opposite is knocked out. The *ronin* are the most famous of Japanese heroes: they were like the "masterless men" of the sagas, and I once saw the word defined as "landless men, masterless men, men like the waves of the sea."

The little boy who speaks The Truth has had his father, his sister, and his dog killed in one of the early fire-raids on London, and has been taken to the country, to a sort of mental institution for children.

CONTENTS

II

BOMBERS

THE CARRIERS

PRISONERS

CAMPS AND FIELDS

SELECTED

POEMS

I

LIVES

A GIRL IN A LIBRARY

An object among dreams, you sit here with your shoes off
And curl your legs up under you; your eyes
Close for a moment, your face moves toward sleep . . .
You are very human.
                    But my mind, gone out in tenderness,
Shrinks from its object with a thoughtful sigh.
This is a waist the spirit breaks its arm on.
The gods themselves, against you, struggle in vain.
This broad low strong-boned brow; these heavy eyes;
These calves, grown muscular with certainties;
This nose, three medium-sized pink strawberries
—But I exaggerate. In a little you will leave:
I'll hear, half squeal, half shriek, your laugh of greeting—
Then, *decrescendo*, bars of that strange speech
In which each sound sets out to seek each other,
Murders its own father, marries its own mother,
And ends as one grand transcendental vowel.

(Yet for all I know, the Egyptian Helen spoke so.)
As I look, the world contracts around you:
I see Brünnhilde had brown braids and glasses
She used for studying; Salome straight brown bangs,
A calf's brown eyes, and sturdy light-brown limbs
Dusted with cinnamon, an apple-dumpling's . . .
Many a beast has gnawn a leg off and got free,
Many a dolphin curved up from Necessity—
The trap has closed about you, and you sleep.
If someone questioned you, *What doest thou here?*
You'd knit your brows like an orangoutang
(But not so sadly; not so thoughtfully)
And answer with a pure heart, guilelessly:
I'm studying. . . .
                        If only you were not!
Assignments,
                recipes,
                        the *Official Rulebook*
Of Basketball—ah, let them go; you needn't mind.
The soul has no assignments, neither cooks
Nor referees: it wastes its time.
                                It wastes its time.
Here in this enclave there are centuries
For you to waste: the short and narrow stream
Of Life meanders into a thousand valleys
Of all that was, or might have been, or is to be.
The books, just leafed through, whisper endlessly . . .
Yet it is hard. One sees in your blurred eyes
The "uneasy half-soul" Kipling saw in dogs'.
One sees it, in the glass, in one's own eyes.
In rooms alone, in galleries, in libraries,
In tears, in searchings of the heart, in staggering joys
We memorize once more our old creation,

Humanity: with what yawns the unwilling
Flesh puts on its spirit, O my sister!

So many dreams! And not one troubles
Your sleep of life? no self stares shadowily
From these worn hexahedrons, beckoning
With false smiles, tears? . . .
                              Meanwhile Tatyana
Larina (gray eyes nickel with the moonlight
That falls through the willows onto Lensky's tomb;
Now young and shy, now old and cold and sure)
Asks, smiling: "But what is she dreaming of, fat thing?"
I answer: She's not fat. She isn't dreaming.
She purrs or laps or runs, all in her sleep;
Believes, awake, that she is beautiful;
She never dreams.
                    Those sunrise-colored clouds
Around man's head—that inconceivable enchantment
From which, at sunset, we come back to life
To find our graves dug, families dead, selves dying:
Of all this, Tanya, she is innocent.
For nineteen years she's faced reality:
They look alike already.
                          They say, man wouldn't be
The best thing in this world—and isn't he?—
If he were not too good for it. But she
—She's good enough for it.
                            And yet sometimes
Her sturdy form, in its pink strapless formal,
Is as if bathed in moonlight—modulated
Into a form of joy, a Lydian mode;
This Wooden Mean's a kind, furred animal
That speaks, in the Wild of things, delighting riddles

To the soul that listens, trusting . . .

                              Poor senseless Life:
When, in the last light sleep of dawn, the messenger
Comes with his message, you will not awake.
He'll give his feathery whistle, shake you hard,
You'll look with wide eyes at the dewy yard
And dream, with calm slow factuality:
"Today's Commencement. My bachelor's degree
In Home Ec., my doctorate of philosophy
In Phys. Ed.

                    [Tanya, they won't even *scan*]
Are waiting for me. . . ."

                              Oh, Tatyana,
The Angel comes: better to squawk like a chicken
Than to say with truth, "But I'm a *good* girl,"
And Meet his Challenge with a last firm strange
Uncomprehending smile; and—then, then!—see
The blind date that has stood you up: your life.
(For all this, if it isn't, perhaps, life,
Has yet, at least, a language of its own
Different from the books'; worse than the books'.)
And yet, the ways we miss our lives are life.
Yet . . . yet . . .

                    to have one's life add up to *yet!*

You sigh a shuddering sigh. Tatyana murmurs,
"Don't cry, little peasant"; leaves us with a swift
"Good-bye, good-bye . . . Ah, don't think ill of me . . ."
Your eyes open: you sit here thoughtlessly.

I love you—and yet—and yet—I love you.

Don't cry, little peasant. Sit and dream.

One comes, a finger's width beneath your skin,
To the braided maidens singing as they spin;
There sound the shepherd's pipe, the watchman's rattle
Across the short dark distance of the years.
I am a thought of yours: and yet, you do not think . . .
The firelight of a long, blind, dreaming story
Lingers upon your lips; and I have seen
Firm, fixed forever in your closing eyes,
The Corn King beckoning to his Spring Queen.

A COUNTRY LIFE

A bird that I don't know,
Hunched on his light-pole like a scarecrow,
Looks sideways out into the wheat
The wind waves under the waves of heat.
The field is yellow as egg-bread dough
Except where (just as though they'd let
It live for looks) a locust billows
In leaf-green and shade-violet,
A standing mercy.
The bird calls twice, "*Red* clay, *red* clay";
Or else he's saying, "Directly, directly."
If someone came by I could ask,
Around here all of them must know—
And why they live so and die so—
Or why, for once, the lagging heron
Flaps from the little creek's parched cresses
Across the harsh-grassed, gullied meadow
To the black, rowed evergreens below.

They know and they don't know.
To ask, a man must be a stranger—
And asking, much more answering, is dangerous;
Asked about it, who would not repent
Of all he ever did and never meant,
And think a life and its distresses,
Its random, clutched-for, homefelt blisses,
The circumstances of an accident?
The farthest farmer in a field,
A gaunt plant grown, for seed, by farmers,
Has felt a longing, lorn urbanity

Jailed in his breast; and, just as I,
Has grunted, in his old perplexity,
A standing plea.

From the tar of the blazing square
The eyes shift, in their taciturn
And unavowing, unavailing sorrow.
Yet the intonation of a name confesses
Some secrets that they never meant
To let out to a soul; and what words would not dim
The bowed and weathered heads above the denim
Or the once-too-often-washed wash dresses?

They are subdued to their own element.
One day
The red, clay face
Is lowered to the naked clay;
After some words, the body is forsaken. . . .
The shadows lengthen, and a dreaming hope
Breathes, from the vague mound, *Life;*
From the grove under the spire
Stars shine, and a wandering light
Is kindled for the mourner, man.
The angel kneeling with the wreath
Sees, in the moonlight, graves.

THE KNIGHT, DEATH, AND
THE DEVIL

Cowhorn-crowned, shockheaded, cornshuck-bearded,
Death is a scarecrow—his death's-head a teetotum
That tilts up toward man confidentially
But trimmed with adders; ringlet-maned, rope-bridled,
The mare he rides crops herbs beside a skull.
He holds up, warning, the crossed cones of time:
Here, narrowing into now, the Past and Future
Are quicksand.
             A hoofed pikeman trots behind.
His pike's claw-hammer mocks—in duplicate, inverted—
The pocked, ribbed, soaring crescent of his horn.
A scapegoat aged into a steer; boar-snouted;
His great limp ears stuck sidelong out in air;
A dewlap bunched at his breast; a ram's-horn wound
Beneath each ear; a spur licked up and out
From the hide of his forehead; bat-winged, but in bone;
His eye a ring inside a ring inside a ring
That leers up, joyless, vile, in meek obscenity—
This is the devil. Flesh to flesh, he bleats
The herd back to the pit of being.

In fluted mail; upon his lance the bush
Of that old fox; a sheep-dog bounding at his stirrup,
In its eyes the cast of faithfulness (our help,
Our foolish help); his dun war-horse pacing
Beneath in strength, in ceremonious magnificence;
His castle—some man's castle—set on every crag:
So, companioned so, the knight moves through this world.
The fiend moos in amity, Death mouths, reminding:

He listens in assurance, has no glance
To spare for them, but looks past steadily
At—at—
                a man's look completes itself.

The death of his own flesh, set up outside him;
The flesh of his own soul, set up outside him—
Death and the devil, what are these to him?
His being accuses him—and yet his face is firm
In resolution, in absolute persistence;
The folds of smiling do for steadiness;
The face is its own fate—*a man does what he must*—
And the body underneath it says: *I am.*

THE FACE

Die alte Frau, die alte Marschallin!

Not good any more, not beautiful—
Not even young.
This isn't mine.
Where is the old one, the old ones?
Those were mine.

It's so: I have pictures,
Not such old ones; people behaved
Differently then . . . When they meet me they say:
You haven't changed.
I want to say: You haven't looked.

This is what happens to everyone.
At first you get bigger, you know more,
Then something goes wrong.
You are, and you say: I am—
And you were . . . I've been too long.

I know, there's no saying no,
But just the same you say it. No.
I'll point to myself and say: I'm not like this.
I'm the same as always inside.
—And even that's not so.

I thought: If nothing happens . . .
And nothing happened.
Here I am.
        But it's not *right*.
If just living can do this,
Living is more dangerous than anything:

It is terrible to be alive.

LADY BATES

The lightning of a summer
Storm wakes, in her clay cave
At the end of the weeds, past the mock-orange tree—
Where she would come bare-footed, curled-up-footed
Over the green, grained, rotting fruit
To eat blackberries, a scratched handful—
The little Lady Bates.
You have played too long today.
Open your eyes, Lady.
                              Is it a dream
Like the ones your mother used to talk away
When you were little and thought dreams were real?
Here dreams are real.
There are no more dreams, no more real—
There is no more night, there is no more day.

When the Lord God and the Holy Ghost and the Child Jesus
Heard about you, Lady,
They smiled all over their faces
And sang like a quartet: "Lady Bates,
Is it you, the little Lady Bates
Our minister, one Sunday evening,
Held down in the river till she choked
In a white dress like an angel's, red
With the clay of that red river? Lady,
Where are the two we sent to fetch your soul:
One coal-black, one high-yellow angel?
Where is night, where is day?
Where are you, Lady Bates?"

They looked for you east, they looked for you west,
And they lost you here in the cuckoo's nest
Eating the sweet white heart of the grass. . . .
You died before you had even had your hair straightened
Or waited on anybody's table but your own.
You stood there helping your step-mother
Boil clothes in the kettle in the yard,
And heard the girls go by, at play,
Calling to you in their soft mocking voices:
"Lady-Bug, Lady-Bug, fly away home."

You are home.
There is a bed of your own
Here where a few stones
Stick up in the tall grass dried to hay—
And one willow, at the end of summer,
Rustles, too dry to weep for you,
And the screech-owl sheers away
And calls, *Who, who*—you are afraid
And he is afraid: who else could see
A black ghost in the dark?
A black, barefooted, pigtailed, trifling ghost
With eyes like white clay marbles,
Who haunts no one—who lies still
In the darkness, waiting
While the lightning-bugs go on and off?
The darning-needles that sew bad girls' mouths shut
Have sewn up your eyes.
If you could open your eyes
You would see nothing.
                    Poor black trash,
The wind has blown you away forever
By mistake; and they sent the wind to the chain-gang

And it worked in the governor's kitchen, a trusty for life;
And it was all written in the Book of Life;
Day and Night met in the twilight by your tomb
And shot craps for you; and Day said, pointing to your soul,
"This *bad* young colored lady,"
And Night said, "Poor little nigger girl."

But Death, after the habit of command,
Said to you, slowly closing his hand:
"You're a big girl now, not even afraid
Of the dark when you awake—
When the day you sleep through
Is over, and you awake,
And the stars rise in the early evening
An inch or two over the grass of your grave—
Try to open your eyes;
Try to reach to one, to the nearest,
Reach, move your hand a little, try to move—
You can't move, can you?
You can't move. . . .
You're fast asleep, you're fast asleep."

WHEN I WAS HOME LAST CHRISTMAS . . .

When I was home last Christmas
I called on your family,
Your aunts and your mother, your sister;
They were kind as ever to me.

They told me how well I was looking
And clearly admired my wife;
I drank tea, made conversation,
And played with my bread, or knife.

Your aunts seemed greyer; your mother's
Lame unexpecting smile
Wandered from doily to doily;
Your dead face still

Cast me, with parted lips,
Its tight-rope-walker's look. . . .
But who is there now to notice
If I look or do not look

At a photograph at your mother's?
There is no one left to care
For all we said, and did, and thought—
The world we were.

A CONVERSATION WITH
THE DEVIL

Indulgent, or candid, or uncommon reader
—I've some: a wife, a nun, a ghost or two—
If I write for anyone, I wrote for you;
So whisper, when I die, *We was too few;*
Write over me (if you can write; I hardly knew)
That I—that I—but anything will do,
I'm satisfied. . . . And yet—

　　　　　　　　　　and yet, you *were* too few:
Should I perhaps have written for your brothers,
Those artful, common, unindulgent others?

Mortal men, man! mortal men! So says my heart
Or else my belly—some poor empty part.
It warms in me, a dog beside a stove,
And whines, or growls, with a black lolling smile:
I never met the man I didn't love.
Life's hard for them . . . these mortals . . . Lie, man, lie!
Come, give it up—this whining poetry;
To any man be anything. If nothing works,
Why then, Have Faith.

　　　　　　　　That blessed word, Democracy!

But this is strange of you: to tempt me now!
It brings back all the past: those earliest offers
—How can I forget?—EACH POEM GUARANTEED
A LIE OR PERMANENTLY IRRELEVANT.
WE FURNISH POEMS *AND* READERS. What a slogan!
(I had only to give credit to "my daemon";
Say, confidentially, "dictated by the devil.")

I can still see my picture in that schoolroom.
And next—who has it now?—*The World's Enormity*,
That novel of the Wandering Jewess, Lilith,
Who went to bed with six millennia.
(It came complete with sales, scenario,
And testimonials of grateful users:
Not like a book at all. . . . Beats life. . . .)

> Beats life.

How ill we knew each other then! how mockingly
I nodded, "Almost thou persuadest me,"
And made my offer:

> "If ever I don't say
To the hour of life that I can wish for: *Stay,
Thou art so fair!* why, you may have my—
Shadow."

> Our real terms were different
And signed and sealed for good, neither in blood
Nor ink but in my life: *Neither to live
Nor ask for life*—that wasn't a bad bargain
For a poor devil of a poet, was it?
One makes a solitude and calls it peace.
So you phrased it; yet—yet—one is paid:
To see things as they are, to make them what they might be—
Old Father of Truths, old Spirit that Accepts—
That's something. . . . If, afterwards, we broke our bargain—

He interrupts: *But what nobility!
I once saw a tenor at the* Opéra Comique
*Who played the Fisher—of Pearls or else of Souls.
He wore a leopard-skin, lay down, and died;
And sang ten minutes lying on his side
And died again; and then, applauded,
Gave six bows, leaning on his elbow,*

And at the seventh started on his encore.
He was, I think, a poet.
                                    Renounce, renounce,
You sing in your pure clear grave ardent tones
And then give up—whatever you're afraid to take,
Which is everything; and after that take credit
For dreaming something else to take its place.
Isn't what is already enough for you?
Must you always be making *something?*
Must each fool cook a lie up all his own?
You beings, won't even being disgust you
With causing something else to be? Make, make—
You squeak like mice; and yet it's all hypocrisy—
How often each of you, in his own heart,
Has wiped the world out, and thought afterwards:
No need to question, now: *"If others are, am I?"*
Still, I confess that I and my good Neighbor
Have always rather envied you existence.
Your simple conceits!—but both of us enjoy them:
"Dear God, make me Innocent or Wise,"
Each card in the card-catalogue keeps praying;
And dies, and the divine Librarian
Rebinds him—
                        rebinds? that's odd; but then, He's odd
And as a rule—
                        I'm lying: there's no rule at all.
The world divides into—believe me—facts.

I see the devil can quote Wittgenstein.
He's blacker than he's painted.
                                    Old ink-blot,
What are you, after all? A parody.

You can be satisfied? then how can I?
If you accept, is not that to deny?
A Dog in a tub, who was the Morning Star!
To have come down in the universe so far
As here, and now, and *this*—and all to buy
One bored, stoop-shouldered, sagging-cheeked particular
Lest the eternal bonfire fail—
                              ah Lucifer!

But at *blacker* an embarrassed smile
Wavers across his muzzle, he breaks in:
It's odd that you've never guessed: I'm through.
To tempt, sometimes, a bored anachronism
Like you into—but why should I say what?
To stretch out by the Fire and improvise:
This pleases me, now there's no need for me.
Even you must see I'm obsolescent.
A specialist in personal relations,
I valued each of you at his own worth.
You had your faults; but you were bad at heart.
I disliked each life, I assure you, for its own sake.
—But to deal indifferently in life and death;
To sell, wholesale, piecemeal, annihilation;
To—I will not go into particulars—
This beats me.
              To men, now, I should give advice?
I'm vain, as you know; but not ridiculous.
Here in my inglenook, shy, idle, I conclude:
I never understood them: as the consequence
They end without me. . . .
                          "Scratch a doctor
And find a patient," I always used to say.

Now that I've time, I've analyzed myself
And find that I am growing, or have grown—
Was always, perhaps, indifferent.
It takes a man to love or hate a man
Wholeheartedly. And how wholeheartedly
You act out All *that is deserves to perish!*
As if to take me at my word—an idle mot
That no one took less seriously than I.
It was so, of course; and yet—and yet—

I find that I've grown used to you. Hell gives us habits
To take the place of happiness, alas!
When I look forward, it is with a pang
That I think of saying, "My occupation's gone."

But twelve's striking: time to be in bed.

I think: He's a changed—all this has shaken him.
He was always delicate: a spirit of society,
A way to come to terms—

                    now, no more terms!

Those pleasant evenings of denunciation!
How gratefully, after five acts' rejection,
A last firm shake and quaver and statistic,
He'd end, *falsetto:* "But let's be realistic"—
Had he, perhaps, exaggerated? He had exaggerated . . .
How quietly, a little later, he'd conclude:
"I accept it all."

                  And now to be unable
To accept, to have exaggerated—

                        to do anything:

It's hard for him. How often he has said,
"I like you for always doing as you please"—
He couldn't. Free will appealed so much to him;
He thought, I think: *If they've the choice . . .*

He was right. And now, to have no choice!

NOLLEKENS

(*In England during the last part of the eighteenth century there
lived a very small, very childish man—a bad speller and a worse
miser—who was the most famous portrait sculptor of his day. He
had a dog called Cerberus, a cat called Jenny Dawdle, servants
called Bronze and Mary Fairy, and a wife named Mary Welch. All
that my poem says that he did, he did; I read about it in* NOLLE-
KENS AND HIS TIMES, *the book "the little Smith" wrote after Nollekens had died.*)

Old Nollekens? No, Little Nollekens:
The Sculptor-Man. "Stand here and you will see
Nine streets commence," he told the little Smith,
Who counted them; "my mother showed them me."
He pricked the King's nose with the calipers.

He stood on King Street in his blue striped hose
And an old bag-wig—the true Garrick-cut—
And stated, in the voice of Samuel Johnson:
"Well, Mrs. Rapsworth, you have just done right.
I wore a pudding as a little boy;
My mother's children all wore puddings."
But Johnson said to him, once: "Bow-wow-wow!"

Dog-Jennings, Shakespeare Steevens, the Athenian
Stuart—these, these too, recalled with joy
The unique power of a Mr. Rich
Who scratched his ear with one foot, like a dog.
It took as much wit as the *are-bolloon*.

The milk-maids danced on May-day, and were paid;
The butchers' snow-house was signed: *Nollekens;*

He stole the nutmegs from the R. A.'s punch—
And once gave Cerberus but half his paunch
And told him, "You have had a roll today."
But Mary Fairy scolded Nollekens,
And old Bronze put her arm around his neck
And asked him how he did. Said Nollekens,
"What! now you want some money—I've got none.
Can you dance?" "Dance, Sir! why, to be sure I can.
Give me the cat." While he watched Jenny Dawdle,
His tabby, dancing round the room with Bronze,
The tears of pleasure trickled down his cheeks
Upon his bib.
                    And yet one day he fell
Into a passion with this favorite cat
For biting the old feather of a pen
He kept to oil the hinges of the gate.
(He showed it to her, and explained to her
The mischief she had done.) So, catching rats,
He stuffed the rat-trap with a pound of cheese
To catch them all at once; so, from the Tower
He went to model George, and cried: "They've got
Such lions there! The biggest did roar so;
My heart, he did roar so." The Sculptor roared.

In winter, when the birds fell from the branches,
In winter, when his servant fed the beggars,
His wife called, "Betty! Betty! Give them this.
Here is a bone with little or no meat upon it."
One, looking at the other steadfastly,
Repeated: "Bill, we are to have a bone
With little or no meat upon it."
                    So.

He left two hundred thousand pounds—and two
Old shoes, the less worn of his last two pairs;
One night-cap, two shirts, and three pairs of stockings;
And the coat in which he married Mary Welch.

Was "Mrs. White delivered of a sun"?
Who measured the dead Pitt? Ah, Nollekens,
To smuggle lace in busts! To leave poor Bronze
But twenty pounds! And yet, whoever dies?

"Ring a bell, ring a bell, my pretty little maid?—
Why, that I will." And I see straining for it
The crescent, tiptoe Nollekens. . . . "My heart,
To sit there in the dark, to save a candle—"
I grieve; but he says, looking steadfastly,
"If you laugh, I'll make a fool of ye."
And I nod, and think acquiescingly:
"Why, it is Nollekens the Sculptor."

SEELE IM RAUM

It sat between my husband and my children.
A place was set for it—a plate of greens.
It had been there: I had seen it
But not somehow—but this was like a dream—
Not seen it so that I knew I saw it.
It was as if I could not know I saw it
Because I had never once in all my life
Not seen it. It was an eland.
An eland! *That* is why the children
Would ask my husband, for a joke, at Christmas:
"Father, is it Donner?" He would say, "No, Blitzen."
It had been there always. Now we put silver
At its place at meals, fed it the same food
We ourselves ate, and said nothing. Many times
When it breathed heavily (when it had tried
A long useless time to speak) and reached to me
So that I touched it—of a different size
And order of being, like the live hard side
Of a horse's neck when you pat the horse—
And looked with its great melting tearless eyes
Fringed with a few coarse wire-like lashes
Into my eyes, and whispered to me
So that my eyes turned backward in their sockets
And they said nothing—
                              many times
I have known, when they said nothing,
That it did not exist. If they had heard
They *could* not have been silent. And yet they heard;
Heard many times what I have spoken
When it could no longer speak, but only breathe—

When I could no longer speak, but only breathe.

And, after some years, the others came
And took it from me—it was ill, they told me—
And cured it, they wrote me: my whole city
Sent me cards like lilac-branches, mourning
As I had mourned—
                and I was standing
By a grave in flowers, by dyed rolls of turf,
And a canvas marquee the last brown of earth.

It is over.
It is over so long that I begin to think
That it did not exist, that I have never—
And my son says, one morning, from the paper:
"An eland. Look, an eland!"
                    —It was so.

Today, in a German dictionary, I saw *elend*
And the heart in my breast turned over, it was—

It was a word one translates *wretched*.

It is as if someone remembered saying:
"This is an antimacassar that I grew from seed,"
And this were true.
                And, truly,
One could not wish for anything more strange—
For anything more. And yet it wasn't *interesting* . . .
—It was worse than impossible, it was a joke.

And yet when it was, I *was*—
Even to think that I once thought

That I could see it is to feel the sweat
Like needles at my hair-roots, I am blind

—It was not even a joke, not even a joke.

Yet how can I believe it? Or believe that I
Owned it, a husband, children? Is my voice the voice
Of that skin of being—of what owns, is owned
In honor or dishonor, that is borne and bears—
Or of that raw thing, the being inside it
That has neither a wife, a husband, nor a child
But goes at last as naked from this world
As it was born into it—

And the eland comes and grazes on its grave.

                        This is senseless?
Shall I make sense or shall I tell the truth?
Choose either—I cannot do both.

I tell myself that. And yet it is not so,
And what I say afterwards will not be so:
To be at all is to be wrong.
                        Being is being old
And saying, almost comfortably, across a table
From—
        from what I don't know—
                                in a voice
Rich with a kind of longing satisfaction:
"To own an eland! That's what I call life!"

THE NIGHT BEFORE THE NIGHT
BEFORE CHRISTMAS

(1934)

In the Arden Apartments
Only a community center and an apartment
From the new lots and the old forest
Of Hillsboro Manor
Lived a girl and her father,
Her aunt, and her one brother.
Nights, warm in her bed,
The girl would still dream of the mother
Who, two years dead,
Looks more like her sister than her mother
—So they had said—
And lays, slowly, a dark shining head
On the dark, stooped shoulder
Of the girl's new teacher.
Is there any question?
The girl has forgotten to answer
And watches him open the door of the cab
That is bringing an Invitation to the Dance:
Till Mother disappears in fur,
The girl trails toward the house
And stares at her bitten nails, her bare red knees—
And presses her chapped, cold hands together
In a middy blouse.

The night before the night before Christmas
Her brother looked out over the snow
That had fallen all day, and saw her

At last, two floors below,
And knocked at the window—drawn-over, frosted-over—
Till she waved and made an O
With her mouth—she was calling.
As she climbed the stairs the snow
Stopped falling, she saw from the landing
Past the big old houses, the small new houses,
And the wood's scrambled boughs
The sun in the hills. . . .

                              Home, home.
She throws her books on the sofa,
And the boy, from his bed,
Calls to her: "Mother, what is snow?"
She answers: "It is the cotton-wool, my Son,
That is falling from the ears of God."
The boys says: "Ho ho ho!
But tell me, Mother,
Why does He keep it in His ears?"
She answers:
"My Son, that He may not hear
How hideously men use His name."

The boy calls, "No, *mis*use, *mis*use!"
She says, "It's just the same."
But she says to herself as she turns on the light in her room:
"How hideously men use His name. . . ."

And she and her father eat dinner with her aunt
And she carries a tray to her brother;
She can hear carols from the radio
In the living-room, as she looks for the dominoes.
After that she offers to read her brother
Another chapter from *The Iron Heel*.

"No, read me from *Stalky*."
She starts to, but says, "When I was your age
I read it all the time." He answers, "It's not real."
She cries, "Oh *isn't* it! Why, in Germany—"
But she stops and finally says, "Well . . ."
And reads about Regulus leaving, full of courage,
For that nigger Manchester, Carthage.
She reads it, *that Negro Manchester*,
But it's just the same, he doesn't understand.
She laughs, and says to her brother:
"Engels lived in Manchester."
The boy says: "Who was Engels?"
She says: "Don't you even remember *that?*"

In her room that night she looks at herself in the mirror
And thinks: "Do I really look like *that?*"
She stares at her hair;
It's really a beautiful golden—anyway, yellow:
She brushes it with affection
And combs her bang back over so it slants.
How white her teeth are.
A turned-up nose . . .
No, it's no use.
She thinks: What do I *really* look like?
I don't know.

Not really.
               Really.

Some dolls and a letter sweater
And a beige fur bear,
A Pink and a Golden and a Blue
Fairy Book, all, all in a row,

Beam from the light, bright, white-starred blue
Of the walls, the clouding curtains—
Anachronisms
East of the sun and west of the moon.
She wraps in white tissue paper
A shiny *Coming Struggle for Power*
For her best friend—
And ties it, one gold, gritty end
Of the string in her mouth, and one in her left hand;
Her right forefinger presses down the knot. . . .
She wraps some improving and delightful
Things she has got for her brother
And one medium-sized present for her aunt
And the gloves she has knitted, the tie she has picked
For her father—poor Lion,
Poor Moose.
She'd give him something that means something
But it's no use:
People are so *dumb*.
She thinks with regretful indignation:
"Why, he might as well not be alive . . ."
And sees all the mottoes at his office,
Like *Do It Now*
And *To Travel Hopefully*
Is A Better Thing Than To Arrive.

Still, he was sorry when my squirrel . . .
He was sorry as Brother when my squirrel . . .
When the gifts are wrapped she reads.

Outside, the wind is—whatever it is;
Inside, it is its own old
Terrible comfortable self:

A ghost in a story—it is all a story.
An uneasy, rocking, comfortable tune
Keeps singing itself under the cold words
In her warm head—cold world
In her warm head—
                              in Praise of Learning:
    LEARN it, WOmen in KITCHens . . .
    LEARN it, MEN of SEVenty . . .
She goes on turning
The big small-printed pages—
A kind of world . . .
                              Use-, surplus-, and exchange-
Value (all these, and plain
Value)
Creak slowly by, the wagon groans—
Creak by, like rags, like bottles—
Like rags, like bottles, like old bones . . .
The bones of men. Her breath is quickened
With pitying, indignant pain.
She thinks: *That's* funny . . .
That's funny: a *Cyclopean* machine . . .
It blinks at her with one blind eye.
Who put your eye out?
                              No one.
Watching with parted lips,
A shy sidelong stare,
She makes out, far off, among columns
Of figures, the children laboring:
A figure buried among figures
Looks at her beggingly, a beast in pain.
She puts her hand
Out into the darkness till it touches:
Her flesh freezes, in that instant, to the iron

And pulls away in blood.
The tears of pain,
Of her own passive, guilty, useless pain
Swell in her eyes, she blinks them over and over
 LEARN it, MEN of SEVen
By your mothers, in the mills—
 WHAT you don't LEARN yourSELF you don't KNOW.

She thinks of her brother going down
To the pits with the ponies, too soon for the sun,
And coming back black, too late for the sun—
No school—he wouldn't even know
Who God is, like the one
In the book—
    not even know
Enough not to believe in God . . .
She thinks, as she has thought,
Her worn old thought,
By now one word:
"But how could this world be
If he's all-powerful, all-good?
No—there's no God."

She reads.

The figures, the values, the one Value
Are clothed with the cloud of her breathing—
The voice echoing over
The dark, stooped shoulder
Ends, hissing a little: "is un*just*."
The hiss blurs in her head
With the hiss of her slow breath,
The lumps of her feet, her lashes

Stuck fast together, washed shut forever, on the wave
Of . . . that is washing, over and over, on the shore
Of . . . something . . . Something . . .
                              But her head jerks straight,
The song strengthens, its last words strike home:
    YOU must be READy to take POWer!
    YOU must be READy to take POWer!

She is reading a Factory Act, a girl in a room.

And afterwards—the room is getting colder
And she is too tired to hold her head up any longer—
She puts away her book
And gives her hair its counted-off
Strokes, and works in and wipes off
Some cold cream from her jar
Of Rexall's Theatrical Cold Cream; and puts on, yawning
Over and over, her boy's blue silk pajamas,
Her white birthday Angora
Bed-socks. She puts up the window—
Her radiator clanks a minute
As someone in the basement banks
The furnace for the night—
And she puts out the light.

She lies half-in, half-out of moonlight
In the sheer cold of the fresh
Sheets, under the patched star-pattern
Of the quilt; and, curled there, warms a world
Out slowly, a wobbling blind ellipse
That lengthens in half a dozen jumps
Of her numb shrinking feet,
Steadies . . . A train wails, over and over,

At a crossing. "It's like Martha,"
She mumbles. "So's the radiator."
The long, mourning, hollow questions
Of Martha Locomotive-Engineer
(You can't get more than a snore
From Martha Janitor, asleep by now
On his brass bed in the basement)
Vex Mary, in her bed-socks, listening guiltily
To the hollow answers of her Lord.
The poor, the poor . . .

                        Her wandering mind
Comes to what was a joy,
What is a sorrow—
A cave opening into the dark
Earth, down to the dead:
What, played with day after day,
Stroked, called to, fed
In the small, wild, straggling park—
Told of, night after night, to the boy
Who listened, longing, among the games
Strewn on his rumpled bed—

                  was gone, one winter day.
She thought: "Tomorrow
He will be where he always is"; and tomorrow
She thought: "He will be here again, tomorrow.
He is asleep with all the other squirrels
There in the hollow of his favorite tree.
He is living on all the nuts he hid
In his cave in the hollow tree."

On warm days, all that winter,
All the warm days of the spring,
She saw the others—never hers;

She thought, trying not to think, "Why, *anything*
Could have happened to him"; she thought, as the living
Think of their life, "Oh, it's not *right!*"
The squirrels are chattering
From leaf to leaf, as her squirrel chattered:
The Poor, the Poor . . .
They have eaten, rapidly,
From her hand, as though to say:
"But you won't hurt me, will you? *Will you?*"

They have nothing to lose but their lives.
She looks home into
The lancing eyes
In the rat-like face, the sucking
Fish-hooks of the little paws: a clawed
Rat with an Angora tail. A clawed
Dead rat with an Angora tail.

There is something deep
Under her will, against her will,
That keeps murmuring to her, "It's so";
And she murmurs, almost asleep:
"Un*just*—no, it's not *so.*
If he were educated . . ."
She sees six squirrels in a row
Thinking in chorus, in slow, low,
Hissing, radiator-steam-valve voices:
"Wherefore Art Thou, Romeo?"
The big squirrel says, "No.
No, that is not *just* it.
Try it again."
Their skein-silk lashes
Tremble, and they look sidelong up at her—

And cry, softly, in their sly,
Dumb, scared, malicious pain . . .
And try it again.

A dream, a dream.
She whispers: "I'm awake.
No, I'm not dreaming, I'm awake."
There is no more moonlight.
Out there, there is darkness and light,
The cold of night.
The world is no longer hidden
By the fire of her lit room,
By the day of the light of the sun.
Out there nothing moves except with a faint
Choked straining shiver;
Sounds except with a faint
Choked croaking sigh.
They are all there together.

Up over
The last twig, in the wild still sky,
Far under the last root, in the wild still sky,
There is another galaxy
Of so many hundreds of thousands of stars
So many hundreds of thousands of years
Away; and it is one
Of so many hundreds of thousands
Of galaxies—some like our own.
It is good, it is evil?
The girl gives her long straining sigh—
In the cells of the needles of the branches
Of the evergreens, the sap is ice.
Wherever the girl stares—

Hung out over, hung in under
The abyss that is her home—
There is something, something: the universe
Is a mirror backed with black
Out of which her face shines back
In the midst of hundreds of millions of suns.

They are all there together.

In the fields outside
There is not one step on the snow,
And each bough is bent with the burden
That is greater, almost, than it can bear.
The breaths of a world are webs
Of angelhair,
Of glass spun, life by life,
Into the trees' earned, magic tinsel.
A handful
Of snowflakes falls from a branch to a bush;
A star hovers
At the tip of a frozen spruce.
It disappears.
(At the side of the shepherds Hänsel
Stands hand in hand with Gretel
And sparkles, under a sparkling star,
Like Lot's own wife:
Bushes, bushes.)
When the owl calls nothing answers.
In the owl's lungs, strained through feathers,
A breath is the edge of a knife. . . .
The haze of the girl's slow breaths,
Of her spun-sugar, cotton-candy breath,

Floats up, clouding the printed stars
Of the faint walls: white
As the down of the wing of an angel; white
As the beard of Friedrich Engels. . . .

In the fields there is not one angel.
In all these fields
There is not one thing that knows
It is almost Christmas.
                              Staring, staring
At the gray squirrel dead in the snow,
She and her brother float up from the snow—
The last crumbs of their tears
Are caught by the birds that are falling
To strew their leaves on the snow
That is covering, that has covered
The play-mound under the snow. . . .
The leaves are the snow, the birds are the snow,
The boy and girl in the leaves of their grave
Are the wings of the bird of the snow.
But her wings are mixed in her head with the Way
That streams from their shoulders, stars like snow:
They spread, at last, their great starry wings
And her brother sings, "I am dying."

"No: it's not so, not so—
Not *really*,"
She thinks; but she says, "You are dying."
He says, "I didn't know."

And she cries: "I don't know, I don't know, I don't know!"

They are flying.

They look down over the earth.
There is not one crumb.
The rays of the stars of their wings
Strike the boughs of the wood, and the shadows
Are caught up into the night,
The first faint whisper of the wind:
Home, home, whispers the wind;
There are shadows of stars, a working
Hand in the . . .

There are words on the graves of the snow.
She whispers, "When I was alive,
I read them all the time.
I read them all the time."
And he whispers, sighing:
"When I was alive . . ."

And, moving her licked, chapped, parted lips,
She reads, from the white limbs' vanished leaves:
To End Hopefully
Is A Better Thing—
                    A Far, Far Better Thing—
It is a far, far better thing . . .

She feels, in her hand, her brother's hand.
She is crying.

DREAM-WORK

A SICK CHILD

The postman comes when I am still in bed.
"Postman, what do you have for me today?"
I say to him. (But really I'm in bed.)
Then he says—what shall I have him say?

"This letter says that you are president
Of—this word here; it's a republic."
Tell them I can't answer right away.
"It's your duty." No, I'd rather just be sick.

Then he tells me there are letters saying everything
That I can think of that I want for them to say.
I say, "Well, thank you very much. Good-bye."
He is ashamed, and turns and walks away.

If I can think of it, it isn't what I want.
I want . . . I want a ship from some near star

To land in the yard, and beings to come out
And think to me: "So this is where you are!

Come." Except that they won't do,
I thought of them. . . . And yet somewhere there must be
Something that's different from everything.
All that I've never thought of—think of me!

THE BLACK SWAN

When the swans turned my sister into a swan
    I would go to the lake, at night, from milking:
The sun would look out through the reeds like a swan,
    A swan's red beak; and the beak would open
And inside there was darkness, the stars and the moon.

Out on the lake a girl would laugh.
    "Sister, here is your porridge, sister,"
I would call; and the reeds would whisper,
    "Go to sleep, go to sleep, little swan."
My legs were all hard and webbed, and the silky

Hairs of my wings sank away like stars
    In the ripples that ran in and out of the reeds:
I heard through the lap and hiss of water
    Someone's "Sister . . . sister," far away on the shore,
And then as I opened my beak to answer

I heard my harsh laugh go out to the shore
    And saw—saw at last, swimming up from the green
Low mounds of the lake, the white stone swans:
    The white, named swans . . . "It is all a dream,"
I whispered, and reached from the down of the pallet

To the lap and hiss of the floor.
    And "Sleep, little sister," the swans all sang
From the moon and stars and frogs of the floor.
    But the swan my sister called, "Sleep at last, little sister,"
And stroked all night, with a black wing, my wings.

THE VENETIAN BLIND

It is the first day of the world
Man wakes into: the bars of the blind
And their key-signature, a leaf,
Stream darkly to two warmths;
One trembles, becomes his face.
He floats from the sunlight
Into a shadowed place:
There is a chatter, a blur of wings—
But where is the edge of things?
Where does the world begin?

His dreams
Have changed into this day, this dream;
He thinks, "But where am I?"
A voice calls patiently:
"Remember."
He thinks, "But where am I?"
His great limbs are curled
Through sunlight, about space.
What is that, *remember?*
He thinks that he is younger
Than anything has ever been.
He thinks that he is the world.

But his soul and his body
Call, as the bird calls, their one word—
And he remembers.

He is lost in himself forever.

And the Angel he makes from the sunlight

Says in mocking tenderness:
"Poor stateless one, wert thou the world?"
His soul and his body
Say, "What hast thou made of us, thy servants?
We are sick. We are dull. We are old."
"Who is this man? We know him not," says the world.

They have spoken as he would have made them speak;
And who else is there to speak?

The bars of the sunlight fall to his face.

And yet something calls, as it has called:
"But where am *I?* But where am *I?*"

A QUILT-PATTERN

The blocked-out Tree
Of the boy's Life is gray
On the tangled quilt: the long day
Dies at last, after many tales.
Good me, bad me, the Other
Black out, and the humming stare
Of the woman—the good mother—
Drifts away; the boy falls
Through darkness, the leagues of space
Into the oldest tale of all.

All the graves of the forest
Are opened, the scaling face
Of a woman—the dead mother—
Is square in the steam of a yard
Where the cages are warmed all night for the rabbits,
All small furry things
That are hurt, but that never cry at all—
That are skinned, but that never die at all.
Good me, bad me
Dry their tears, and gather patiently
Through the loops of the chicken-wire of the cages
Blackberries, the small hairy things
They live on, here in the wood of the dream.

Here a thousand stones
Of the trail home shine from their strings
Like just-brushed, just-lost teeth.
All the birds of the forest
Sit brooding, stuffed with crumbs.

But at home, far, far away
The white moon shines from the stones of the chimney,
His white cat eats up his white pigeon.

But the house hums, "We are home." Good me, bad me
Sits wrapped in his coat of rabbit-skin
And looks for some little living thing
To be kind to, for then it will help him—
There is nothing to help; good me
Sits twitching the rabbit's-fur of his ears
And says to himself, "My mother is basting
Bad me in the bath-tub—"
                              the steam rises,
A washcloth is turned like a mop in his mouth.
He stares into the mouth
Of the whole house: there in it is waiting—
No, there is nothing.

He breaks a finger
From the window and lifts it to his—
"Who is nibbling at me?" says the house.
The dream says, "The wind,
The heaven-born wind";
The boy says, "It is a mouse."
He sucks at the finger; and the house of bread
Calls to him in its slow singing voice:
"Feed, feed! Are you fat now?
Hold out your finger."
The boy holds out the bone of the finger.
It moves, but the house says, "No, you don't know.
Eat a little longer."
The taste of the house
Is the taste of his—

"I don't know,"
Thinks the boy. "No, I don't *know!*"

His whole dream swells with the steam of the oven
Till it whispers, "You are full now, mouse—
Look, I have warmed the oven, kneaded the dough:
Creep in—ah, ah, it is warm!—
Quick, we can slip the bread in now," says the house.
He whispers, "I do not know
How I am to do it."

                    "Goose, goose," cries the house,
"It is big enough—just look!
See, if I bend a little, so—"

He has moved. . . . He is still now, and holds his breath.
If something is screaming itself to death
There in the oven, it is not the mouse
Nor anything of the mouse's. Bad me, good me
Stare into each other's eyes, and timidly
Smile at each other: it was the Other.

But they are waking, waking; the last stair creaks—
Out there on the other side of the door
The house creaks, "How is my little mouse? Awake?"
It is she.
He says to himself, "I will never wake."
He says to himself, not breathing:
"Go away. Go away. Go away."

And the footsteps go away.

THE ISLAND

"While sun and sea—and I, and I—
Were warped through summer on our spar,
I guessed beside the fin, the gull,
And Europe ebbing like a sail
A life indifferent as a star.

"My lids were grating to their close,
My palms were loosening to die,
When—failing through its drift of surf,
Whale-humped, its beaches cracked with salt—
The island gave its absent sigh.

"Years notched my hut, my whiskers soughed
Through summer's witless stare: blue day
Flickered above the nothingness
That rimmed me, the unguessed abyss
Broke on my beaches, and its spray

"Frosted or salted with its curling smile
The printless hachures of the sand . . .
I lay with you, Europe, in a net of snows:
And all my trolls—their noses flattened into Lapps'
Against the thin horn of my windows—wept;

"Vole, kobold, the snowshoe-footed hare
—Crowned with the smoke of steamboats, shagg'd with stars—
Whispered to my white mistress: *He is Mars;*
Till I called, laughing: *Friends! subjects! customers!*
And her face was a woman's, theirs were men's.

"All this I dreamed in my great ragged bed . . .
Or so I dreamed. The dawn's outspeaking smile
Curled through my lashes, felled the Märchen's wood;
The sun stripped my last cumulus of stars,
And the sea graved all the marshes of the swan.

"So, so. The years ticked past like crabs
Or an hour inched out to heaven, like the sea.
One day, by my black hand, my beard
Shone silver; I looked in astonishment
And pinched my lean calves, drawn with many scars,

"With my stiff fingers, till the parrot called
In my grum, quavering voice: *Poor Robinson!*
My herd came bleating, licked my salty cheeks;
I sobbed, and petted with a kind of love
These joys of mine—the old, half-human loves

"That had comforted my absent life . . .
I have dreamed of men, and I am old.
There is no Europe." The man, the goats, the parrot
Wait in their grove for death; and there floods to them
In its last thundering spray, the sea, the sea!

IN THE WARD:
THE SACRED WOOD

The trees rise from the darkness of the world.
The little trees, the paper grove,
Stand woodenly, a sigh of earth,
Upon the table by this bed of life
Where I have lain so long: until at last
I find a Maker for them, and forget
Who cut them from their cardboard, brushed
A bird on each dark, fretted bough.
But the birds think and are still.
The thunder mutters to them from the hills
My knees make by the rainless Garden.
If the grove trembles with the fan
And makes, at last, its little flapping song
That wanders to me over the white flood
On which I float enchanted—shall I fall?
A bat jerks to me from the ragged limb
And hops across my shudder with its leaf
Of curling paper: have the waters gone?
Is the nurse damned who looked on my nakedness?
The sheets stretch like the wilderness
Up which my fingers wander, the sick tribes,
To a match's flare, a rain or bush of fire
Through which the devil trudges, coal by coal,
With all his goods; and I look absently
And am not tempted.
Death scratches feebly at this husk of life
In which I lie unchanging, Sin despairs
Of my dull works; and I am patient . . .
A third of all the angels, in the wars

Of God against the Angel, took no part
And were to God's will neither enemies
Nor followers, but lay in doubt:
                                    but lie in doubt.

There is no trade here for my life.
The lamb naps in the crèche, but will not die.
The halo strapped upon the head
Of the doctor who stares down my throat
And thinks, "Die, then; I shall not die"—
Is this the glitter of the cruze of oil
Upon the locks of that Anointed One
Who gazes, dully, from the leafless tree
Into the fixed eyes of Elohim?
I have made the Father call indifferently
To a body, to the Son of Man:
"It is finished." And beneath the coverlet
My limbs are swaddled in their sleep, and shade
Flows from the cave beyond the olives, falls
Into the garden where no messenger
Comes to gesture, "Go"—to whisper, "He is gone."

The trees rise to me from the world
That made me, I call to the grove
That stretches inch on inch without one God:
"I have unmade you, now; but I must die."

THE WIDE PROSPECT

THE ORIENT EXPRESS

One looks from the train
Almost as one looked as a child. In the sunlight
What I see still seems to me plain,
I am safe; but at evening
As the lands darken, a questioning
Precariousness comes over everything.

Once after a day of rain
I lay longing to be cold; and after a while
I was cold again, and hunched shivering
Under the quilt's many colors, gray
With the dull ending of the winter day.
Outside me there were a few shapes
Of chairs and tables, things from a primer;
Outside the window
There were the chairs and tables of the world. . . .
I saw that the world
That had seemed to me the plain

Gray mask of all that was strange
Behind it—of all that *was*—was all.

But it is beyond belief.
One thinks, "Behind everything
An unforced joy, an unwilling
Sadness (a willing sadness, a forced joy)
Moves changelessly"; one looks from the train
And there is something, the same thing
Behind everything: all these little villages,
A passing woman, a field of grain,
The man who says good-bye to his wife—
A path through a wood full of lives, and the train
Passing, after all unchangeable
And not now ever to stop, like a heart—

It is like any other work of art.
It is and never can be changed.
Behind everything there is always
The unknown unwanted life.

A GAME AT SALZBURG

A little ragged girl, our ball-boy;
A partner—ex-Afrika-Korps—
In khaki shorts, P. W. illegible.
(He said: "To have been a prisoner of war
In Colorado iss a *privilege*.")
The evergreens, concessions, carrousels,
And D. P. camp of Franz Joseph Park;
A gray-green river, evergreen-dark hills.
Last, a long way off in the sky,
Snow-mountains.

Over this clouds come, a darkness falls,
Rain falls.
                On the veranda Romana,
A girl of three,
Sits licking sherbet from a wooden spoon;
I am already through.
She says to me, softly: *Hier bin i'*.
I answer: *Da bist du.*

I bicycle home in my raincoat
Through the ponchos and pigtails of the streets,
Bathe, dress, go down four flights of stairs
Past Maria Theresa's sleigh
To the path to the garden, walk along the lake
And kick up, dreamily, the yellow leaves
Of the lindens; the pigeons are cooing
In the morning-glories of the gardener's house,
A dragonfly comes in from the lake.
The nymphs look down with the faces of Negroes,

Pocked, moled with moss;
The stone horse has sunk in marsh to his shoulders.

But the sun comes out, and the sky
Is for an instant the first rain-washed blue
Of becoming: and my look falls
Through falling leaves, through the statues'
Broken, encircling arms
To the lives of the withered grass,
To the drops the sun drinks up like dew.

In anguish, in expectant acceptance
The world whispers: *Hier bin i'*.

AN ENGLISH GARDEN
IN AUSTRIA

(seen after DER ROSENKAVALIER*)*

It is as one imagined it: an English garden . . .

Mein Gott!—as all the little girls here say—
To see here the path, the first step of that first path
Our own great parents took! Today, *le Roi Soleil* shines
On his mistress's nuns' orphans' *Athalie;*
Saint-Simon, Leibnitz, and some wandering stars
Murmuring for joy together . . . and in the night
A Ruin, a Prospect, and one blasted tree
Lour on their progress; and next day where are they?

On such a path as this, a "rustic beau
[Or bear; one's doubtful, with this orchestration]
Of thirty-five" pauses to hear a man
Reciting in a big fur hat, with feeling—
And growls politely, "Metastasio?"
They whisper: "Quiet! That's J. J. Rousseau,"
And bear him off to the measures of a *Ländler.*
Helped to his coach, the Baron exits grumbling
About the "luck of all us Lerchenaus."

. . . It was not thus that you sang, Farinelli!
By graver stages, up a sterner way,
You won to those fields the candelabra lit,
Paused there; sang, as no man since has sung—
A present and apparent deity—the pure
Impossible airs of Arcady: and the calm

Horsehair-wigged shepherds, Gods of that Arcadian
Academy, wept inextinguishable tears.

Such power has music; and the repeated spell
Once a day, at evening, opened the dull heart
Of old mad Philip: all his courtiers wept
And the king asked, weeping: "Why have I wept?"
And Farinelli sang on; Ferdinand
Buried his father, ruled—
                    and heard, paused, heard again:
The years went on, men withered, Farinelli sang.

You are silent now: you, Faustina Hasse,
Her husband Johann Adolf, the Abate
Metastasio . . . very silent.
They float past; seem to whisper, to the oat
Of a shepherd wintering very far from Weimar:
"We also have dwelt in Arcady."
                    —So Death.

The shades of your Grotto have encompassed me.
How can I make out, among these ruins, your Ruin?
You went for this pleasing terror to the past
And built it here, an image of the Possible:
Well ruined, Ruin! . . .
                    But I come late.

In those years Europe lived beneath the lightning
Of the smile of that certain, all too certain spirit
Whom Almighty God—
                    whom *le bon Dieu* sent for a rod
To these Philistines; he held out sixty years,
Gentling savage Europe with his Alexandrines,

Submitted, went up to Switzerland, and perished.
One spends one's life with fools, and dies among watches.
But see him in flower, in a Prussian garden.
He walks all summer, yawning, in the shade
Of an avenue of grenadiers; and a Great Person
In a tie-wig walks with this monkey, tags his verses,
And—glancing sideways, with suspicion—speaks of *Götz
Von Berlichingen mit der eisernen Hand.*
Said Frederick: "Here's the hand, but where's the glove?"
Or words to that effect; and next year jailed him
For having gone off with his (Pharaoh's) flute
In a sack of corn upon a baggage-camel.
Or words to that effect . . . Then all the world
Shifts to another gear: Count Almaviva and his valet
Shake hands, cry *Citoyen!* are coffined by a sad
Danton; assisting, Anacharsis Clootz—
To the Masons' Funeral Music of their maker.
And one might have seen, presiding among drummers,
An actress named *Raison* (*née* Diderot).
Meanwhile Susanna and the Countess sigh
For someone not yet on the scene; their man of tears
Retires, is rouged as Destiny: Rousseau
Comes in as Cain, upon a charger . . . Instead of his baton
This corporal carries *Werther* in his knapsack.
He reads it seven times, and finds no fault
Except with Werther: he was too ambitious.
The soldier nods—these buzzing Mamelukes
Have made him drowsy; shadows darken all the East
And over his feeling shoulder, as he sleeps,
Die Weltgeschichte peeps down upon his Sorrows.
(He wakes, smiles sleepily, and tweaks its ear.)
At Jena he shows his gratitude, says: "Here's a man!"
(What were the others? . . .

Dead men. He'd killed them every one.)
A vulgar demon, but our own: he still prepares us
"Plays worthy of the savages of Canada"—
Up from the floorboards soars the infernal
Everything that is deserves to perish,
And actors, author, audience die applauding.
Then he whispers, winking: "Politics is Destiny!"
And some *Spiessbürger*, some *aquarelliste*,
Some *Spielverderber* from a Georgian seminary
Echo him—higher, higher: *"Es muss sein!"*

"Others have understood the world; we change it."
"Truth is what works." "I have seen the Future and it works."

No Lerchenau was e'er a spoilsport,
A ghost sings; and the ghosts sing wonderingly:
Ist halt vorbei! . . . Ist halt vorbei! . . .

Then there is silence; a soft floating sigh.
Heut' oder morgen kommt der Tag,
And how shall we bear it?
                                    Lightly, lightly.

The stars go down into the West; a ghostly air
Troubles the dead city of the earth.

. . . It is as one imagined it: an English garden.

A SOUL

It is evening. One bat dances
Alone, where there were swallows.
The waterlilies are shadowed
With cattails, the cattails with willows.

The moon sets; after a little
The reeds sigh from the shore.
Then silence. There is a whisper,
"Thou art here once more."

In the castle someone is singing.
"Thou are warm and dry as the sun."
You whisper, and laugh with joy.
"Yes, here is one,

"Here is the other . . . *Legs* . . .
And they move so?"
I stroke the scales of your breast, and answer:
"Yes, as you know."

But you murmur, "How many years
Thou hast wandered there above!
Many times I had thought thee lost
Forever, my poor love.

"How many years, how many years
Thou hast wandered in air, thin air!
Many times I had thought thee lost,
My poor soul, forever."

A RHAPSODY ON IRISH THEMES

At six in the morning you scratched at my porthole,
Great-grandmother, and looked into my eyes with the eyes
Of a potato, and held out to me—only a dollar—
A handkerchief manufactured with their own hands
By the Little People; a *Post* wet from no earthly press,
Dreamed over the sinking fire
                              of a pub by a Papal Count.
Look: a kerchief of linen, embroidered cunningly
In the green of Their hearts, in Their own hand:
A SOUVENIR OF OLD IRELAND.

Then you turned into the greatest of the gulls
That brood on the seesaw green
Swells of the nest of the harbor of Cóbh.

All is green, all is small, all is—
It is not; the nuns sailing to Ireland
Disembark, and are dovetailed into the black
Nuns sailing from Ireland: a steady state,
But black. And that patch of the red of blood
On the hillside without any trees, by the topless
Tower, is a Cardinal surely? the steak
This Lady with Cromwell's sword in her suitcase
Wolfs for her lonely supper, with a sigh
Like an empire falling? And the sky is the blue
Of the fat priest's brimmed beret,
Of the figuring and clasps of his new
Accordion (that plays all night, by itself, like the sword
Of a hero, a *Mother Machree*

That'd tear your heart out entirely).

The soft, guileful, incessant speech
Plaits into the smack of the feet
In their dance on the deck, every night in the moonlight;
The smile is, almost, the smile
Of the nuns looking on in delight—
The delight of a schoolgirl at recess, a trouble to no one.
But—blue eyes, gray face—
I was troubled by you.

               The old woman, met in sleep,
Skinned herself of her wrinkles, smiled like a goddess—
Skinned herself of the smile, and said to me softly:
"There's no rest for you, grandson, till you've reached the
    land
Where, walking the roads with an adding-machine on your
    shoulder,
You meet no one who knows it."
                     Well, I hold nothing
Against you but what you are. One can almost bear
The truth in that soft shameless speech
That everything is a joke—from your Sublime
To your Ridiculous is one false step—
But one settles at birth on that step of the stair
And dislikes being shown that there's nothing there.
But I believe you: the orchestration
Of this world of man is all top or bottom,
And the rest is—
              anything that you say.
To argue longer would be un-Irish,
Unnatural grandson that I am!

—Great-grandson.

Old sow, old Circe, *I'm* not your farrow.
Yet ah, to be eaten! There honk beside me the Tame Geese
Of the Seven Hills of the City of Dublin,
And it's Stentor I cough like, what with the smoke of peat—
Man is born to Ireland as the sparks fly upward:
A sleepwalker fallen from the edge of Europe,
A goosegirl great among publicans and censors.

—She speaks, smiling, of someone "who felt at home
In whatever was least like home, and fell in love
With the world for not being America"—
                    Old Sibyl!
It's your last leaf . . . Still, play it: it is so;
I'm from nowhere, I'm Nobody. But if I'm to be reminded
By any nobody—
                    Ireland, I've seen your cheeks
The red of dawn: the capillaries are broken.

Long ago, the sun set. These are the Western Isles.

                    —And, waking, I saw on the Irish Sea
Orion, his girdle a cinch, and himself a hunter,
An Irish hunter . . .
                    that is to say, a horse.

Great-grandmother, I've dreamed of you till I'm hoarse.
It was all a lie: I take back every word.
                    . . . If your shin *is* speckled,
Your grin, alas! pious—
                    still, what a brow-ridge!
You Eden of Paleolithic survivals,

You enclave of Brünn and of Borreby man,
Fold your child home, when—weary of Learning—
He sighs for the Night of the Spirit of Man.

. . . What have I said! Faith, I'm raving entirely:
Your taste is like lotus, you Irish air!
Get the wax out of your ears, you oarsmen,
We sail at six . . . And here's the last lesson
I learned from you, Ireland:

                         what it is I've forgotten.

Well, what if it's gone? Here're some verses of Goethe's—
An old upright man, a lover of Ireland—
You Senate of Ireland, to straighten the conduct
Of such of your people as need it: *In peace*
                         Keep tidy
                         Your little coops.
                         In war
                         Get along
                         With quartered troops.

THE MEMOIRS OF GLÜCKEL
OF HAMELN

We are all children to the past.
Here where no knowledge is sufficient
Even the wise are satisfied with shards
That add at best into an almanac,
And two treaties and a bust afford
The worst fool an hypothesis
A bee would groan all year to check.
"Historians—bad men!—come black as miners
From History; their tongues are dry with Fact;
And ah! their faces do not shine like mine,"
One judges from the armchair of a brain
Or avoids seldom, and with careful pains.
One touch of insight makes the ages kin,
And nothing helps like ignorance to apply it.

The skull one starts at, a carving
(One swims with a flashlight to the cave)
That bulks in the poor light like a senator
Are—not history, merely data,
The discrete and uninstructed facts.
But if one learns little from them, still
One emerges, sometimes, skeptical
Of a little one has known before.

Poor Glückel, mostly I was bored:
The deals all ended in a gain or anguish
Explained and disregarded with a text;
Money and God were too immediate,
The necessities that governed every act.

One marries, one has children whom one marries;
One's husband dies; one mourns, re-marries.
The reader reads, reads, and at last, grown weary
With hearing the amount of every dowry,
He mumbles, Better to burn than marry . . .
Yet when I think of those progressive years,
Of Newton, Leibnitz, Mandeville, and Pope,
You lend a certain body to the thought;
I am perplexed with your fat tearful ghost.
I hear you in the plague: "See, see, she plays
And eats a buttered roll, as nicely as you please . . ."
One can do nothing with these memories.
They are as stubborn, almost, as our lives'.

One goes along the corridor; and, outside certain years,
One hears, if one listens hard, a small
Vivacious sound, a voice that is not stilled.
It speaks as it used to speak—speaks uselessly
As a voice can speak; and if one should enter,
The room is dark, and the dark is empty.
The voice has a hollow sound, without you. Glückel,
The one thing missing in your book is you;
But how can we miss it, we who never knew you?
But we miss it, somehow; and, somehow, we knew you.
We take your place as our place will be taken.
The butter is oily on the roll, and the child plays
As nicely as you please—as nicely as we please.

TO THE NEW WORLD

(For an emigrant of 1939)

In that bad year and city of your birth
They traded bread for bank-notes weight for weight,
And nothing but the statues kept the smile
The waltzers wore once: excluding, innocent,
The face of old and comfortable injustice.
And if you wept,
Dropped red into a city where the husbandless
And fatherless were weeping too, who cared
For one more cry or one more child? You grew,

Time put words into your mouth, and you put sugar
Upon your windowsill and waited for a brother—
The stork was greedy, ate, brought nothing in return.
But your life was thinking of you, took you back to Prague,
At school there, timid, boisterous, you spoke
The unaccustomed Czech—
The children laughed at you. For you were learning
New words and a new life, the old
City and its new country too were learning
An old wish: to be just; yes, to be free.

"I saw summer in my time." Summer is ending.
The storms plunge from the tree of winter, death
Moves like an impulse over Europe. Child,
What man is just or free?—but fortunate,
Warm in time's hand, turning and trusting to his face;
And that face changes.
Time is a man for men, and He is willing
For many a new life, for others death. Already

He buys His trench-coat, falls, writes His big book;

Points here, points here: to Jews, to wicked friends—
His words are the moments of a man's life . . .
And now the men march. One morning you awoke
And found Vienna gone, your father said:
"Us next!" And you were next.
Us next!
Cried map and mouth, oppressors and oppressed,
The appeasers as they gave you—but you were gone.
"I had a speech, a city." *What is your name?*
"My name is what my name was." *You have no name.*

So the dream spoke to you: in Zurich, Paris,
In London on a lawn. The unbefriending sea
Cried to you, "Stranger!" Superb, inhospitable,
The towers of the island turned their gaze
Past the girl who looked to the great statue:
So green, so gay . . .
That is how you came. Your face shows white
Against the dark time, your words are indistinct,
One cry among so many, lost in the sound

Of degradation and of agony, the peoples dying.
The net was laid for you, and you are free.
Past the statue there is summer, and the summer smiles
The smile of justice or injustice: blind,
Comfortable, including. Here are the lives
And their old world;
Far off, inside you, a conclusive face
Watches in accusation, in acceptance. It is He.
You escaped from nothing: the westering soul
Finds Europe waiting for it over every sea.

THE MÄRCHEN

(GRIMM'S TALES)

Listening, listening; it is never still.
This is the forest: long ago the lives
Edged armed into its tides (the axes were its stone
Lashed with the skins of dwellers to its boughs);
We felled our islands there, at last, with iron.
The sunlight fell to them, according to our wish,
And we believed, till nightfall, in that wish;
And we believed, till nightfall, in our lives.

The bird is silent; but its cold breast stirs
Raggedly, and the gloom the moonlight bars
Is blurred with the fluff its long death strewed
In the crumpled fern; and far off something falls.
If the firs forget their breath, if the leaf that perishes
Holds, a bud, to spring; sleeps, fallen, under snow—
It is never still. The darkness quakes with blood;
From its pulse the dark eyes of the hunter glow
Green as their forest, fading images
Of the dream in the firelight: shudder of the coals
In their short Hell, vined skeleton
Of the charcoal-burner dozing in the snow.
Hänsel, to map the hard way, cast his bones
Up clouds to Paradise; His sparrows ate
And he plunged home, past peat and measures, to his kin
Furred in the sooty darkness of the cave
Where the old gods nodded. How the devil's beard
Coiled round the dreaming Hänsel, till his limbs
Grew gnarled as a fakir's on the spindling Cross

72

The missions rowed from Asia: eternal corpse
Of the Scapegoat, gay with His blood's watered beads,
Red wax in the new snow (strange to His warmed stare);
The wooden mother and the choir of saints, His stars;
And God and His barons, always, iron behind.
Gorged Hänsel felt His blood burn thin as air
In a belly swollen with the airy kine;
How many ages boiled Christ's bark for soup!
Giddy with emptiness, a second wife
Scolding the great-eyed children of a ghost,
He sends them, in his tale, not out to death
(Godfather Death, the reaping messenger),
Nor to the devil cringing in the gloom,
Shifting his barred hooves with a crunch like snow—
But to a king: the blind untroubled Might
Renting a destiny to men on terms—
Come, mend me and wed half of me, my son!
Behind, the headsman fondles his gnawn block.
So men have won a kingdom—there are kings;
Are giants, warlocks, the unburied dead
Invulnerable to any power—the Necessity
Men spring from, die under: the unbroken wood.

Noon, the gold sun of hens and aldermen
Inked black as India, on the green ground,
Our patterns, homely, mercenary, magnified—
Bewitching as the water of Friar Bacon's glass.
(*Our* farmer fooled the devil with a turnip,
Our tailor won a queen with seven flies;
Mouser and mousie and a tub of fat
Kept house together—and a louse, a louse
Brewed small beer in an eggshell with a flea.)
But at evening the poor light, far-off, fantastic—

Sun of misers and of mermen, the last foolish gold
Of soldiers wandering through the country with a crutch—
Scattered its leagues of shadows on the plots
Where life, horned sooty lantern patched with eyes,
Hides more than it illumines, dreams the hordes
Of imps and angels, all of its own hue.
In the great world everything is just the same
Or just the opposite, we found (we never went).
The tinkers, peddlers brought their pinch of salt:
In our mouths the mill of the unresting sea
Ground till their very sores were thirsty.
Quaking below like quicksand, there is fire—
The dowser's twig dips not to water but to Hell;
And the Father, uncomfortable overseer,
Shakes from the rain-clouds Heaven's branding bolt.
Beyond, the Alps ring, avalanche on avalanche,
And the lost palmers freeze to bliss, a smile
Baring their poor teeth, blackened as the skulls
Of sanctuaries—splinters of the Cross, the Ark, the Tree
Jut from a saint's set jawbone, to put out
With one bought vision many a purging fire.
As the circles spread, the stone hopes like a child.
The weak look to the helpless for their aid—
The beasts who, ruled by their god, Death,
Bury the son with their enchanted thanks
For the act outside their possibility:
The victim spared, the labors sweated through, for love
Neither for mate nor litter, but for—anything.
When had it mattered whom we helped? It always paid.
When the dead man's heart broke they found written there
(He could not write): *The wish has made it so.*
Or so he wished. The platter appliquéd
With meals for parents, scraps for children, gristle

For Towser, a poor dog; the walnut jetting wine;
The broom that, fretting for a master, swept a world;
The spear that, weeping for a master, killed a child;
And gold to bury, from the deepest mines—
These neither to wisdom nor to virtue, but to Grace,
The son remembered in the will of God—
These were wishes. The glass in which I saw
Somewhere else, someone else: the field upon which sprawled
Dead, and the ruler of the dead, my twin—
Were wishes? Hänsel, by the eternal sea,
Said to the flounder for his first wish, *Let me wish*
And let my wish be granted; it was granted.
Granted, granted. . . . Poor Hänsel, once too powerless
To shelter your own children from the cold
Or quiet their bellies with the thinnest gruel,
It was not power that you lacked, but wishes.
Had you not learned—have we not learned, from tales
Neither of beasts nor kingdoms nor their Lord,
But of our own hearts, the realm of death—
Neither to rule nor die? to change, to change!

HOHENSALZBURG: FANTASTIC VARIATIONS ON A THEME OF ROMANTIC CHARACTER

I should always have known; those who sang from the river,
Those who moved to me, trembling, from the wood
Were the others: when I crushed on a finger, with a finger,
A petal of the blossom of the lime, I understood
(As I tasted, under the taste of the flower, the dark
Taste of the leaf, the flesh that has never flowered)
All the words of the wood but a final word:
Pure, yearning, unappeasable—
A word that went on forever, like the roar
The peoples of the bees made in the limes.

When they called from the rushes I heard you answer:
I am a dweller of the Earth.

The old woman who sat beside her wheel
In her cottage under the hill, and gave you tea
When the mist crept up around her, evenings,
And you came to her, slowly, out of the mist
Where you had run, all evening, by the shore
Naked, searching for your dress upon the sand—
She would say to you, each evening: "What you do will do,
But not forever . . .
                    What you want is a husband and children."
And you would answer: *They will do,*
But not forever.
                    The old woman,
The stone maid sunk in the waters of the Earth
Who murmured, "You too are fair—

Not so fair as I, but fair as I was fair—"
These said to you, softly: "You are only a child.
What would you be, if you could have your wish?
You are fair, child, as a child is fair.
How would you look, if you could have your wish?"
You answered:
                I would be invisible.

When I woke it was still night.
I saw, as I always saw,
A castle rising above limes—
A castle that has never been taken.
I felt in the map-pocket of the skirt
Of my leather coat, but mice had eaten the bar
Of chocolate, and left me foil like tinsel.
There was moonlight.
At the path out into the wood, a deer
Stood with stars in the branches of its antlers:
An iron deer.
Then there was nothing but night.
I felt at my hand
For an instant, the wing of a swallow—
Your hand opened across my hand.

I reached to you, but you whispered: *Only look.*
I whispered: "I see only moonlight."

I am here behind the moonlight.

You are there.
I thought at first
That you were only a ghost,
A ghost asleep in a castle that is asleep.

But these German ghosts—harsh clumsy things—
Haunt no one, but only change
Men into things, things into things.
Many a chandelier
Clouded with china roses, many a swan
Floating beside its shepherd, among cresses,
Many a star
Set in the antlers of an iron deer
Was once a sleeper wandering through the wood.
Some walked through the pits of the glade to a ghost
And were changed: a ghost wants blood;
And it will do—
                    but not forever.
But I shall be with you here forever:
Past the dust of thorns, past the sleepers wound
Like worms in the terrible chains of their breath,
I shall lie in your arms forever.
If you sleep I shall sleep, if you wake I shall wake,
If you die I shall also die.

You said: *I am then not dead?*
You are only sleeping . . .
When I come to you, sprawled there asleep
At the center of all the webs, at the final
Point of the world: one drop of your blood,
I shall bend to you, slowly—
                    You are asleep.
The leaves breathe with your breath. The last, least stir
Of the air that stumbles through a fur of leaves
Says the sound of your name, over and over, over and over;
But someday—
Years off, many and many years—
I shall come to you there asleep,

I shall take you and . . .
                    Tell me.
No, no, I shall never.
                    Tell me.
You must not know.
                    Tell me.
I—I shall kiss your throat.

My throat?

There, it is only a dream.
I shall not so—I shall never so.

I saw, in your eyes beside my eyes,
A gaze pure, yearning, unappeasable:
Your lips trembled, set
For an instant in the slightest smile
I ever saw;
Your cold flesh, faint with starlight,
Wetted a little with the dew,
Had, to my tongue, the bloom of fruit—
Of the flower: the lime-tree-flower.
And under the taste of the flower
There was the taste of—

I felt in the middle of the circle
Of your mouth against my flesh
Something hard, scraping gently, over and over
Against the skin of my throat.
I woke and fell asleep and woke:
Your face above me
Glowed faintly now—something light, a life
Pulsed there. When I saw that it was my blood,

I used my last strength and, slowly,
Slowly, opened my eyes
And pushed my arms out, that the moonlight pierced and
    held—
I said: "I want you"; and the words were so heavy
That they hung like darkness over the world,
And you said to me, softly: *You must not so.*
I am only a girl.
Before I was a ghost I was only a girl.

I said to you, "Before I was a ghost
I was only a—
                    a ghost wants blood:
When they find me, here except for my blood,
They will search for you all night—harsh clumsy things
In their tunics and leather shorts and pigtails.
All the badges along the bands of their hats will shine. . . .
When all but one has said to you, *Gute Nacht,*
And you have answered, are almost free
To call to me there in the bonds of the moonlight,
The last will mutter cunningly, *Grüss Gott.*
Then as all my blood
Flows from your limbs into your heart—
When, at the name of God,
You can say nothing, O dweller of the Earth—
You will cry out bitterly, and they will seize you
And bind you and boil you to death—the dead also die—
There at the fountain of the square
Just under the castle, by the iron deer;
Make of you a black-pudding, deck it with schillings and
    thaler,
And serve it, all *herrlich,* to the Man of the castle
With a sign stuck on it:

To eat is *verboten*."

Or so it went once: I have forgotten. . . .

What shall I call you, O Being of the Earth?
What I wish you to call me I shall never hear.

We shall change; we shall change; but at last, their stars,
We shall rest in the branches of the antlers
Of the iron deer.
                    But not forever:
Many a star
Has fallen, many a ghost
Has met, at the path to the wood, a ghost
That has changed at last, in love, to a ghost—
We should always have known. In this wood, on this Earth
Graves open, the dead are wandering:
In the end we wake from everything.

Except one word—

In the end one wakes from everything.
                    Except one word
Goes on, always, under the years,
A word we have never understood—
And our life, our death, and what came past our life
Are lost within that steady sound:
Pure, yearning, unappeasable,
The one spell turns above us like the stars.

And yet surely, at the last, all these are one,
We also are forever one:
A dweller of the Earth, invisible.

ONCE UPON A TIME

MOVING

Some of the sky is grey and some of it is white.
The leaves have lost their heads
And are dancing round the tree in circles, dead;
The cat is in it.
A smeared, banged, tow-headed
Girl in a flowered, flour-sack print
Sniffles and holds up her last bite
Of bread and butter and brown sugar to the wind.

Butter the cat's paws
And bread the wind. We are moving.
I shall never again sing
Good morning, Dear Teacher, to my own dear teacher.
Never again
Will Augusta be the capital of Maine.
The dew has rusted the catch of the strap of my satchel
And the sun has fallen from the place where it was chained
With a blue construction-paper chain. . . .

Someone else must draw the bow
And the blunderbuss, the great gobbler
Upside-down under the stone arrow
In the black, bell-brimmed hat—
And the cattycornered bat.
The witch on the blackboard
Says: "Put the Plough into the Wagon
Before it turns into a Bear and sleeps all winter
In your play-house under the catalpa."
Never again will Orion
Fall on my speller through the star
Taped on the broken window by my cot.
My knee is ridged like corn
And the scab peels off it.

We are going to live in a new pumpkin
Under a gold star.

There is not much else.
The wind blows somewhere else.
The brass bed bobs to the van.
The broody hen
Squawks upside down—her eggs are boiled;
The cat is dragged from the limb.
The little girl
Looks over the shoulders of the moving-men
At her own street;
And, yard by lot, it changes.
Never again.
But she feels her tea-set with her elbow
And inches closer to her mother;
Then she shuts her eyes, and sits there, and squashed red
Circles and leaves like colored chalk

Come on in her dark head
And are darkened, and float farther
And farther and farther from the stretched-out hands
That float out from her in her broody trance:
She hears her own heart and her cat's heart beating.

She holds the cat so close to her he pants.

THE SLEEPING BEAUTY:
VARIATION OF THE PRINCE

After the thorns I came to the first page.
He lay there gray in his fur of dust:
As I bent to open an eye, I sneezed.
But the ball looked by me, blue
As the sky it stared into . . .
And the sentry's cuirass is red with rust.

Children play inside: the dirty hand
Of the little mother, an inch from the child
That has worn out, burst, and blown away,
Uncurling to it—does not uncurl.
The bloom on the nap of their world
Is set with thousands of dawns of dew.

But at last, at the center of all the webs
Of the realm established in your blood,
I find you; and—look!—the drop of blood
Is there still, under the dust of your finger:
I force it, slowly, down from your finger
And it falls and rolls away, as it should.

And I bend to touch (just under the dust
That was roses once) the steady lips
Parted between a breath and a breath
In love, for the kiss of the hunter, Death.
Then I stretch myself beside you, lay
Between us, there in the dust, His sword.

When the world ends—it will never end—
The dust at last will fall from your eyes
In judgment, and I shall whisper:
"For hundreds of thousands of years I have slept
Beside you, here in the last long world
That you had found; that I have kept."

When they come for us—no one will ever come—
I shall stir from my long light sleep,
I shall whisper, "Wait, wait! . . . She is asleep."
I shall whisper, gazing, up to the gaze of the hunter,
Death, and close with the tips of the dust of my hand
The lids of the steady—
                    Look, He is fast asleep!

THE PRINCE

After the door shuts, and the footsteps die,
I call out, "Mother?" No one answers.
I chafe my numb feet with my quaking hands
And hunch beneath the covers, in my curled
Red ball of darkness; but the floor creaks, someone stirs
In the other darkness—and the hairs all rise
Along my neck, I whisper: "It is he!"

I hear him breathing slowly, as he bends
Above me; and I pull my eyes
Back into me, and shrink up like the rabbit
They gave me when he— Then he waits, I wait.
I hear his fingers rasping, like five paws,
Up through the dirt, until I cannot breathe
But inch my cold hand out to his cold hand:

Nothing, nothing! I throw off the furs
And sit up shaking; but the starlight bars
A vague window, in the vacant dark
The sentry calls out something, like a song.
I start to weep because—because there are no ghosts;
A man dies like a rabbit, for a use.
What will they pay me, when I die, to die?

THE CARNEGIE LIBRARY,
JUVENILE DIVISION

The soot drifted from the engines to the marble
The readers climbed to: stone, and the sooty casts
(Dark absent properties confused with crates
And rest-rooms in the darkness of a basement,
And constant in their senseless line, like dates:
A past that puzzles no one, or a child)
All overlooking—as the child too overlooked—
The hills and stone and steeples of the town
Grey in the pure red of the dying sun.

Here under the waves' roof, where the seals are men;
In the rhymes' twilight, where the old cup ticks
Its gnawing lesson; where the beasts loom in the green
Firred darkness of the märchen: country the child thought life
And wished for and crept to out of his own life—
Must you still isle such, raiders from a world
That you so long ago lost heart to represent?
The child tugs the strap tight round four books
To leave the cavern. And the cut-out ornaments
In colors harsh and general as names,
The dolls' scarred furniture, too small
For anything but pity, like the child—
Surely you recognize in these the hole
That widens from the middle of a field
To that one country where the poor see gold?
The woodman dances home, rich, rich; but a shade glides
Into the bright strange sunlight of the world
He owned once; the thaler blur out like a tear,

He knocks like a stranger and a stranger speaks,
And he sees, brass on the knocker, the gnome's joyless smile.

The books too read to ashes—for one owns
Nothing, and finds that there is no exchange
For all the uses lined here, free as air,
Fleeting as air: the sad repeated spell
Of that deep string, half music and half pain—
How many have believed you worth a soul!
How many here will purchase with a world
These worlds still smoldering for the perpetual
Children who haunt this fire-sale of the centuries.
Wandering among so many lives, they too will bear
The life from which they cannot yet escape;
And learn to doubt, with our sad useless smile,
That single universe the living share—
The practice with which even the books are charred.

We learned from you so much about so many things
But never what we were; and yet you made us that.
We found in you the knowledge for a life
But not the will to use it in our lives
That were always, somehow, so different from the books'.
We learn from you to understand, but not to change.

THE BLIND SHEEP

The Sheep is blind; a passing Owl,
A surgeon of some local skill,
Has undertaken, for a fee,
The cure. A stump, his surgery,
Is licked clean by a Cat; his tools—
A tooth, a thorn, some battered nails—
He ranges by a shred of sponge
And he is ready to begin.
Pushed forward through the gaping crowd,
"Wait," bleats the Sheep; "is all prepared?"
The Owl lists forceps, scalpel, lancet—
The old Sheep interrupts his answer;
"These lesser things may all be well;
But tell me, friend—how goes the world?"
The Owl says blankly: "You will find it
Goes as it went ere you were blinded."
"What?" cries the Sheep. "Then take your fee
But cure some other fool, not me:
To witness that enormity
I would not give a blade of grass.
I am a Sheep, and not an Ass."

THE SKATERS

I stood among my sheep
As silent as my staff.
Up the sea's massy floor
I saw the skaters pass.

Long as the wind, as light
I flowed upon their track
Until at evening's edge
I marked their breathless flock.

I moved among them then
Like light along its lands,
Lust wreathed their lips, and speed
Stiffened their tissue limbs.

North through the months of night
We skirred along the floes;
The million glances flecked
Upon my flickering gaze

Bent to me in the stars
Of one obsessing face—
The urgent and engrossed,
The fast and flattering glass.

How long we pled our love!
How thorough our embrace!
By post and igloo, we prolonged
The Way and splendors of our kiss

Until at man's last mark
"Here we must pause," I cried,
"To block from the eternal ice
Our shelter from this endless night."

But the iron's dazzling ring, the roar
Of the starred ice black below
Whirl our dazed and headlong strides
Through the whirling night into

The abyss where my deaf limbs forget
The cold mouth's dumb assent—
The skaters like swallows flicker
Around us in the long descent.

JONAH

As I lie here in the sun
And gaze out, a day's journey, over Nineveh,
The sailors in the dark hold cry to me:
"What meanest thou, O sleeper? Arise and call upon
Thy God; pray with us, that we perish not."

All thy billows and thy waves passed over me.
The waters compassed me, the weeds were wrapped about
    my head;
The earth with her bars was about me forever.
A naked worm, a man no longer,
I writhed beneath the dead:

But thou art merciful.
When my soul was dead within me I remembered thee,
From the depths I cried to thee. For thou art merciful:
Thou hast brought my life up from corruption,
O Lord my God. . . . When the king said, "Who can tell

But God may yet repent, and turn away
From his fierce anger, that we perish not?"
My heart fell; for I knew thy grace of old—
In my own country, Lord, did I not say
That thou art merciful?

Now take, Lord, I beseech thee,
My life from me; it is better that I die . . .
But I hear, "Doest thou well, then, to be angry?"
And I say nothing, and look bitterly
Across the city; a young gourd grows over me

And shades me—and I slumber, clean of grief.
I was glad of the gourd. But God prepared
A worm that gnawed the gourd; but God prepared
The east wind, the sun beat upon my head
Till I cried, "Let me die!" And God said, "Doest thou well

To be angry for the gourd?"
And I said in my anger, "I do well
To be angry, even unto death." But the Lord God
Said to me, "Thou hast had pity on the gourd"—
And I wept, to hear its dead leaves rattle—

"Which came up in a night, and perished in a night.
And should I not spare Nineveh, that city
Wherein are more than six-score thousand persons
Who cannot tell their left hand from their right;
And also much cattle?"

SONG: NOT THERE

I went to the cupboard, I opened the door,
I cried to my people, *O it's not there!*
"How long did you think it would last?" said the cook,
Said the butler, "Does anyone care?"
But where is it, where is it? O it's not there,
Not there to be saved, not there to be saved,
If I'm saved it will not be there.

I ran to a plate, to a pig, to a dish,
An old china pig, a plate, to a pear,
Said, *To find it, O, I will look anywhere,*
Said, *Anywhere, Anywhere* . . . "Look anywhere,"
Said the plate as it laughed, "yes, look anywhere;
There's as good as here, there's as good as there—
For where shall you look to be saved?"

I said to my people, the plate, to the cupboard,
The pig on its platter, the pear, the pear:
O where is my salvation?
                          "O it's not anywhere.
You break in my head like a dish," said the plate,
"A pig," said the pig, "a pear," said the pear—
Not there to be saved, go not there to be saved,
If you're saved it will not be there.

CHILDREN SELECTING BOOKS IN A LIBRARY

With beasts and gods, above, the wall is bright.
The child's head, bent to the book-colored shelves,
Is slow and sidelong and food-gathering,
Moving in blind grace . . . Yet from the mural, Care,
The grey-eyed one, fishing the morning mist,
Seizes the baby hero by the hair

And whispers, in the tongue of gods and children,
Words of a doom as ecumenical as dawn
But blanched, like dawn, with dew. The children's cries
Are to men the cries of crickets, dense with warmth
—But dip a finger into Fafnir, taste it,
And all their words are plain as chance and pain.

Their tales are full of sorcerers and ogres
Because their lives are: the capricious infinite
That, like parents, no one has yet escaped
Except by luck or magic; and since strength
And wit are useless, be kind or stupid, wait
Some power's gratitude, the tide of things.

Read meanwhile . . . hunt among the shelves, as dogs do,
  grasses,
And find one cure for Everychild's diseases
Beginning: *Once upon a time there was*
A wolf that fed, a mouse that warned, a bear that rode
A boy. Us men, alas! wolves, mice, bears bore.
And yet wolves, mice, bears, children, gods and men

In slow perambulation up and down the shelves
Of the universe are seeking . . . who knows except them-
selves?
What some escape to, some escape: if we find Swann's
Way better than our own, and trudge on at the back
Of the north wind to—to—somewhere east
Of the sun, west of the moon, it is because we live

By trading another's sorrow for our own; another's
Impossibilities, still unbelieved in, for our own . . .
"I am myself still"? For a little while, forget:
The world's selves cure that short disease, myself,
And we see bending to us, dewy-eyed, the great
CHANGE, dear to all things not to themselves endeared.

THE WORLD
IS EVERYTHING
THAT IS THE CASE

SEARS ROEBUCK

"A passing cyclist winks; well, let her, let her!
If even my baked, cream blinds are alloy,
Slatted to bare me to these lambs of Satan—
My cotton nainsook union suit, my shoes
Elk-tanned, with woodsman's heels and safety toes,
Will sheathe me through the wilds of this bad world.
I write once more for a pronouncing Bible.

"But thumbing these leaves, I light upon a plasterer's hawk,
A wilderness of Women's Intimate Apparel.
A girl slides to me in ribbed flannel panties. . . .
Ah, gauds of earth! My heart catches in my throat:
Beware! the rockets poised above the world!
How even my oilskins, in the evil hour,
Blaze up around me! Ah, the fire, the fire!"

—So John Doe, Don Juan—ah, poor Honest John,
Mailing your endless orders west from Patmos!

A UTOPIAN JOURNEY

"In a minute the doctor will find out what is wrong
And cure me," the patients think as they wait.
They are as patient as their name, and look childishly
And religiously at the circumstances of their hope,
The nurse, the diplomas, the old magazines.

And their childishness is natural; here in this office
The natural perplexities of their existence,
The demands they can neither satisfy nor understand,
Are reduced to the child's, "I hurt," the bare
Intention of any beast: to go on being.

And they go in to the doctor at last
And go out to the hospitals, sanitoria, or graves
He prescribes—look into the masked unnoticing
Faces of their saviors, smell the sick
Sweet smell of nothing, leave, send back their checks;

But what was it? What am I?
The convalescent stitched up with black thread,
His pains withering, his uneasy head
Quieted with enemas and orange-juice, the inconclusive
Evasive silence—remembers, silently, a sweet,

Evasive, and conclusive speech . . . Goes back to his living,
Day and Night ask, *Child, have you learned anything?*
He answers, *Nothing*—walled in these live ends,
In these blind blossoming alleys of the maze
That lead, through a thousand leaves, to the beginning

Or that lead at last into—dark, leaved—a door.

HOPE

*The spirit killeth, but
the letter giveth life.*

The week is dealt out like a hand
That children pick up card by card.
One keeps getting the same hand.
One keeps getting the same card.

But twice a day—except on Saturday—
But every day—except on Sunday—
The wheel stops, there is a crack in Time:
With a hiss of soles, a rattle of tin,
My own gray Daemon pauses on the stair,
My own bald Fortune lifts me by the hair.

*Woe's me! woe's me! In Folly's mailbox
Still laughs the postcard, Hope:
Your uncle in Australia
Has died and you are Pope.
For many a soul has entertained
A Mailman unawares—
And as you cry, Impossible,
A step is on the stairs.*

One keeps getting the same dream
Delayed, marked *Postage Due,*
The bill that one has paid
Delayed, marked *Payment Due*—

Twice a day, in a rotting mailbox,
The white grubs are new:

And Faith, once more, is mine
Faithfully, but Charity
Writes hopefully about a new
Asylum—but Hope is as good as new.

Woe's me! woe's me! In Folly's mailbox
Still laughs the postcard, Hope:
Your uncle in Australia
Has died and you are Pope.
For many a soul has entertained
A Mailman unawares—
And as you cry, Impossible,
A step is on the stairs.

At home, in my flannel gown, like a bear to its floe,
I clambered to bed; up the globe's impossible sides
I sailed all night—till at last, with my black beard,
My furs and my dogs, I stood at the northern pole.

There in the childish night my companions lay frozen,
The stiff furs knocked at my starveling throat,
And I gave my great sigh: the flakes came huddling,
Were they really my end? In the darkness I turned to my rest.

—Here, the flag snaps in the glare and silence
Of the unbroken ice. I stand here,
The dogs bark, my beard is black, and I stare
At the North Pole . . .

                And now what? Why, go back.

Turn as I please, my step is to the south.
The world—my world spins on this final point
Of cold and wretchedness: all lines, all winds
End in this whirlpool I at last discover.

And it is meaningless. In the child's bed
After the night's voyage, in that warm world
Where people work and suffer for the end
That crowns the pain—in that Cloud-Cuckoo-Land

I reached my North and it had meaning.
Here at the actual pole of my existence,
Where all that I have done is meaningless,
Where I die or live by accident alone—

Where, living or dying, I am still alone;
Here where North, the night, the berg of death
Crowd me out of the ignorant darkness,
I see at last that all the knowledge

I wrung from the darkness—that the darkness flung me—
Is worthless as ignorance: nothing comes from nothing,
The darkness from the darkness. Pain comes from the darkness
And we call it wisdom. It is pain.

THE SNOW-LEOPARD

His pads furring the scarp's rime,
Weightless in greys and ecru, gliding
Invisibly, incuriously
As the crystals of the cirri wandering
A mile below his absent eyes,
The leopard gazes at the caravan.
The yaks groaning with tea, the burlaps
Lapping and lapping each stunned universe
That gasps like a kettle for its thinning life
Are pools in the interminable abyss
That ranges up through ice, through air, to night.
Raiders of the unminding element,
The last cold capillaries of their kind,
They move so slowly they are motionless
To any eye less stubborn than a man's. . . .
From the implacable jumble of the blocks
The grains dance icily, a scouring plume,
Into the breath, sustaining, unsustainable,
They trade to that last stillness for their death.
They sense with misunderstanding horror, with desire,
Behind the world their blood sets up in mist
The brute and geometrical necessity:
The leopard waving with a grating purr
His six-foot tail; the leopard, who looks sleepily—
Cold, fugitive, secure—at all that he knows,
At all that he is: the heart of heartlessness.

THE BOYG, PEER GYNT, THE ONE ONLY ONE

"Well, I have had a happy life," said Hazlitt;
Swift's eye was as big as an egg.
What did the Moor say? I forget.
The servant who killed Greville cried.
They all died well: that is, they died.

How can one learn all this from Works?
It wasn't Gulliver the keeper beat;
The informer was impressed with Marx,
Not *Capital*. On the picnics
Those Sundays, no one mentioned politics.

They lived, they died. "I am what I am,"
Someone heard Swift stammer: he was crazy.
Beethoven, dying, learned to multiply.
What does it mean? Why, nothing.
Nothing? . . . How well we all die!

MONEY

I sit here eating milk-toast in my lap-robe—
They've got my nightshirt starchier than I told 'em . . .
  Huh! . . .
I'll tell 'em. . . .
                Why, I wouldn't have given
A wooden nickel to a wooden Indian, when I began.
I never gave a soul a cent that I could help
That I remember: now I sit here hatching checks
For any mortal cause that writes in asking,
And look or don't look—I've been used to 'em too long—
At seven Corots and the Gobelins
And my first Rembrandt I outbid Clay Frick for:
A dirty Rembrandt bought with dirty money—
But nowadays we've all been to the cleaners'.
(Harriet'd call Miss Tarbell Old Tarbaby—
It none of it will stick, she'd say when I got mad;
And she was right. She always was.)
I used to say I'd made my start in railroads
—"Stocks, that is," I'd think and never say—
And made my finish in philanthropy:
To think that all along it'uz Service!
I could have kicked myself right in the face
To think I didn't think of that myself. . . .
"There isn't one of you that couldn't have done what I did—"
That was *my* line; and I'd think: "if you'd been me."
SEES U.S. LAND OF OPPORTUNITY,
A second-page two-column headline,
Was all I got, most years.

           They never knew a thing!

Why, when I think of what I've done, I can't believe it!

. . . A Presbyterian'd say it's Providence.
In my time I've bought the whole Rhode Island Legislature
For—I disremember how much; what for too. . . .
Harriet'd have Nellie Melba in
To entertain our friends—it never entertained *me* none—
And I'd think: "Birdie, I could buy you
The way you'd buy a piece of Melba toast."
I had my troubles—nothing money wouldn't cure.
A percentage of the world resented me
There on my money bags in my silk hat.
(To hear Ward I'd still straw stuck in my fur.)
But in the end the money reconciled 'em all.
Don't someone call it the Great Reconciler?
When my boys dynamited thirteen trestles
On the New York Central, I went against my custom then
And told the papers: "Money's a *responsibility*."

I'd talk down money if I hadn't any. As it was,
The whole office force could hear me through two doors.
E. J. said they said: "Listen to the Old Man go!"

Why, it was money
That got me shut of my poor trusting wife,
And bought my girl from her, and got me Harriet—
What else would Harriet've married *me* for? . . . She's gone
     now
And they're gone too, but it's not gone. . . .
You can take it with you anywhere *I*'m going.

. . . While I was looking up my second son-in-law
In Dun and Bradstreet, the social secretary

Came on him in the *Almanach de Gotha*.
It was like I figured, though: he didn't take.

You couldn't tell my grandson from a Frenchman.

And Senators! . . .
                                    I never saw the man I couldn't buy.

When my Ma died I boarded with a farmer
In the next county; I used to think of her,
And I looked round me, as I could,
And I saw what it added up to: money.
Now I'm dying—I can't call this living—
I haven't any cause to change my mind.
They say that money isn't everything: it isn't;
Money don't help you none when you are sighing
For something else in this wide world to buy. . . .
The first time I couldn't think of anything
I didn't have, it shook me.

                        But giving does as well.

THE EMANCIPATORS

When you ground the lenses and the moons swam free
From that great wanderer; when the apple shone
Like a sea-shell through your prism, voyager;
When, dancing in pure flame, the Roman mercy,
Your doctrines blew like ashes from your bones;

Did you think, for an instant, past the numerals
Jellied in Latin like bacteria in broth,
Snatched for by holy Europe like a sign?
Past sombre tables inched out with the lives
Forgotten or clapped for by the wigged Societies?

You guessed this? The earth's face altering with iron,
The smoke ranged like a wall against the day?
—The equations metamorphose into use: the free
Drag their slight bones from tenements to vote
To die with their children in your factories.

Man is born in chains, and everywhere we see him dead.
On your earth they sell nothing but our lives.
You knew that what you died for was our deaths?
You learned, those years, that what men wish is Trade?
It was you who understood; it is we who change.

VARIATIONS

I

"I lived with Mr. Punch, they said my name was Judy,
I beat him with my rolling-pin, he hit me with his cane.
I ran off with a soldier, he followed in a carriage,
And he drew a big revolver and he shot me through the brain.
But that was his duty, he only did his duty—"

Said Judy, said the Judy, said poor Judy to the string.

"O hear her, just hear her!" the string said softly.
And the string and Judy, they said no more.
Yes, string or Judy, it said no more.
But they hanged Mr. Punch with a six-inch rope,
And "Clap," said the manager; "the play is over."

II

"I lay like a swan upon the down of Heaven.
When the clouds came the rain grew
Into the rice of my palaces, the great wits
Were the zithers of my garden, I stood among sedge
And held to the peoples the gold staff of God."

Said Grace, said Good, O said the son of God.

The wives and wise, the summer's willows
Nodded and were fed by the wind; when the snow fell
And the wind's steps were pink in the pure winter,
Who spared his charcoal for the son of God,
The vain wind failing at the pass to Hell?

III

"I lived in a room full of bears and porridge,
My mother was dead and my nurse was horrid.
I sat all day on a white china chamber
And I lay all night in my trundle bed.
And she wasn't, she wasn't, O not a bit dead!"

The boy said, the girl said—and Nurse she said:

"I'll stew your ears all day, little hare,
Just as God ate your mother, for you are bad,
Are bad, are bad—" and the nurse is the night
To wake to, to die in: and the day I live,
The world and its life are her dream.

IV

"I was born in a hut, my wit is heavy.
My sister died, they killed my father.
There is no time I was not hungry.
They used me, I am dying.
I stand here among graves."

The white, the yellow, the black man said.

And the world said: Child, you will not be missed.
You are cheaper than a wrench, your back is a road;
Your death is a table in a book.
You had our wit, our heart was sealed to you:
Man is the judgment of the world.

LE POÈTE CONTUMACE

(Tristan Corbière)

On the coast of ARMORICA. A monastery.
The winds complained, inside: *Another windmill;*
    All the donkeys of the county
Came to grate their teeth off in the seedy ivy
Of a wall so holey that no living man
      Had ever come in through the doorway.

Alone—but still on its own feet, full of poise,
Corrugated as the jaw of an old woman,
Its roof knocked onto the corner of its ear,
Gaping like a ninny, the tower stood there

As vain as ever: it had its memories. . . .
It wasn't anything but a nest of black sheep,
Lovers from the bush, a rat down on his luck,
Stray dogs, benighted hobos—smugglers and customs-
      inspectors.

One year, the tenant of this low tower
Was a wild poet with a ball in his wing
Fallen among owls: the venerable owls
Who, from some height, considered him.—He respected their
      holes—
He, the only paying owl, as his lease stated:
Twenty-five écus a year: door to be replaced.

As for the people of the place, he didn't see them:
Only, passing by, they looked from below,

Turning their noses up at his window;
The priest guessed that he was a leper;
And the mayor answered: "What can *I* do?
    He's more likely an Englishman . . . some such crea-
        ture."

The women learned—no doubt from the buzzards—
That he *lived in concubinage with the Muses!* . . .
In short, a heretic . . . Some Parisian
From Paris or some such place?—Alas, nobody knew a thing.
He was invisible; and as *his Wenches*
Didn't advertise themselves, nobody said a word.

As for him, he was simply an idler, tall, thin, pale;
An amateur hermit, chased in by a squall. . . .
The far green fields—the feverish ones—he'd loved too well.
Given up by process-servers, by physicians,
He had lit here, fed up, looking for a spot
To die by himself or to live by default. . . .

    Making, from something almost like an artist,
    Something almost like a philosopher;
    Rain or shine, always complaining;
    Off any human track.

There remained to him a hammock, a hurdy-gurdy,
A spaniel who slept under the name of Fido.
No less faithful, sad and sweet as she,
Was another companion: he called it Ennui.

Dying in his sleep, he lived in dreams.
His dreams were the tide that rose on the shore,
    The tide that fell.

Sometimes, vaguely, he took up waiting. . . .
Waiting for what . . . the tide to rise—the tide to fall—
 Someone . . . Who knows?

He knows! . . . Floating in the wind of his watch-tower,
Has he forgotten how quick are the dead?
He? Which *he?* the stray ghost? the dilapidated
Body searching for its own ill-buried spirit?

Surely, She isn't far—She for whom you bellow,
O Stag of St. Hubert! Ah, sad flameless forehead. . . .
Poor old sport, have they dug you up without a permit?
Play dead if you can . . . For She has wept for you!

—But could he, He? Wasn't he a poet . . .
Immortal as any other? . . . And inside his poor head,
His moved-out-of head, he still could feel them,
The hexameters marching their catercornered rounds.

For want of knowing how to live, he kept alive—
For want of knowing how to die, he wrote:

"Dear, this is someone dead for so many ages
In that poet's heart of yours, he's already a myth.
I rhyme, therefore I am . . . but don't be afraid, it's *blank*
—The shell of an oyster torn from its bed!
I've pinched myself all over: it's me. Last mistake
En route to Heaven—for my niche is high as that!—
I asked myself, all ready to take wing:
Heads or tails . . . —And here I am, still asking. . . .

"It was to you I said, *Good-bye to life.*
How you wept! I watched you crying for me

Till it made me want to stay and help you cry.
But it's over now: I'm just a doting ghost,
Some bones and (I was going to say *flesh*). There's no mistake.
It's me all right, here I am—but like an erasure.

"We were connoisseurs of all the curiosities:
Notice this *objet d'art*.—I'm sick of it.—
In my distastes especially, I had good taste.
You know, I have let go of Life with gloves.
The Other one wouldn't touch with tweezers. . . .
I'm looking for *something different* for this—window-
        dummy.

"Come back to me: Your eyes in these eyes here! Your lips
Upon these lips! . . . Feel how hot my face is—here: that's
        You,
It's You I'm sick with . . . Remember?—those nights that
        could have burned
The rainbow out of heaven—
                                    what's become of it? It's charcoal.
And that star? . . . It's no use looking for the star
        You tried to see upon my brow.
        A spider has set its web
        At the same spot—on the ceiling.

"I am a stranger.—Perhaps it's better so.
Isn't it? . . . No, come back and notice me a little.
You always doubted, Thomas: I want to see your faith,
I want to see you touch the wound and whisper:—You!—

"Come finish me off again—it's quite amusing:
You'll see my harvests from your bedroom . . . it's Decem-
        ber;

My great fir-forests, the golden flowers of broom,
My heather of Armorica . . . piled on the andirons.
Come gorge yourself on fresh air. Here there's a breeze
So crisp! . . . the ends of my roof curl.
The sun's so mild . . . it freezes all the time.
The spring . . . —Spring, isn't it your twenty years?
It's you I'm waiting for: look, already a swallow
. . . Nailed to my turret, a rusty swallow.
Soon we can go gathering mushrooms. . . .
On my staircase, gilded . . . by a candle-end.
On the greening wall a dried-up periwinkle
Exists. . . . Then we'll take the waters, lie there drying
On the sand-dunes with the other driftwood.
The sea coos its *Lullaby for Castaways;*
A barcarole at dusk . . . for the wild ducks.

"Like *Paul* and *Virginia*—virginal, if you wish—
We'll graze on the grass of our lost paradise. . . .
Or *Robinson* with *Friday*—why, it's easy:
The rain has made an island of my kingdom.

"But if, near me, you're afraid of being lonely,
We've friends, plain honest ones—a poacher;
Not to count that blue cloak that habitually
Paces its rounds and holds a customs-inspector. . . .
No more process-servers! I've got moonlight,
I've got friends—all poor broke lovesick fools.

—"And our nights! *Whispering I know not what of wild and
        sweet,*
Nights for a Romeo!—Day will never break.—
Aurora awak'ning, burst from the bonds of sleep,
Dropping her white sheet . . . stops up my chimney.

Look, my nightingales! . . . nightingales of the tornado,
Gay as larks, wailing like screech-owls!
My weathercock, way up there, rubs the rust off his yodel,
And you can hear my Aeolian door lamenting
As did Saint Anthony in his temptation . . .
Come, pretty limb of Sata—of seduction!

"Hoy! the rats in the garret are dancing farandoles!
The roof's slates rattle down like castanets!
The witches in my belfry—

                              No, I've not one witch!

"Ah, but wouldn't I retail my skin to Satan
If he'd only tempt me with a little ghost—
You. I see you everywhere, but white as a seer
I worship you . . . And that's pitiful: to worship what one
          loves!
Appear, a dagger in thy heart!—That's it,
You know, like *Inès de La Sierra*. . . .
A knock . . . Someone's there! . . .

                              Alas! it's a rat.

"I daydream . . . and it's always you. On everything
Your memory perches, like a mocking spirit:
My loneliness . . . —*You!*—My owls with golden eyes:
—*You!*—My crazy weathercock: oh, *You!*—Any more?—
—*You!* my shutters flinging their arms out to the storm. . . .
A far-off voice: Your song!—this is ecstasy!
The squalls that beat at Your lost name—this is crazy . . .
Crazy, but it's You! My heart, wide open
          As my own disordered shutters,
          Beats in senseless circles, to the breath
          Of the most fantastic gusts.

"Wait . . . a ready shadow, for an instant, came
To trace your profile on the naked wall,
And I turned my head—to hope or to remember—
Sister Anne, Sister Anne, do you see no one coming?

"No one . . . I see—I see, in my cold chamber,
My bed padded with its push-cart satin
And my dog asleep on it—poor beast—
And I laugh . . . because it makes me a little sick.

"I've used, to summon you, my hurdy-gurdy and my lyre;
My heart's cracked jokes—the imbecile—to fool itself. . . .
Come weep, if my lines have made you laugh;
          Come laugh, if they have made you weep. . . .

"It will be comical. . . . Come play at poverty.
Back to Nature: *Come live with me and be my love.* . . .
It's raining in my hearth, it's raining in my heart:
In my late heart.
                    Come! my candle's out, I've no more fire."

*   *   *

His lamp went out. He opened the window.
The sun was rising. He looked at his letter,
Laughed and tore it up . . . The little white pieces
Seemed, through the fog, a flight of gulls.

THE GRAVES IN
THE FOREST

LA BELLE AU BOIS DORMANT

She lies, her head beneath her knees,
In their old trunk; and no one comes—
No porter, even, with a check
Or forceps for her hard delivery.
The trains pant outside; and she coils breathlessly
Inside his wish and is not waked.

She is sleeping but, alas! not beautiful.
Travelers doze around; are borne away;
And the thorns clamber up her stony veins.
She is irreparable; and yet a state
Asks for her absently, and citizens
Drown for an instant in her papery eyes.

Yet where is the hunter black enough to storm
Her opening limbs, or shudder like a fish
Into the severed maelstrom of her skull?

The blood fondles her outrageous mouth;
The lives flourish in her life, to alienate
Their provinces from her outranging smile.

What wish, what keen pain has enchanted her
To this cold period, the end of pain,
Wishes, enchantment: this suspending sleep?
She waits here to be waked—as he has waited
For her to wake, for her to wake—
Her lips set in their slack conclusive smile.

A STORY

Even from the train the hill looked empty.
When I unpacked I heard my mother say:
"Remember to change your stockings every day—
Socks, I mean." I went on walking past their
Buildings gloomy with no lights or boys
Into the country where the roads were lost.

But when I woke I thought: The roads aren't lost.
That night the buildings were no longer empty
But packed and blazing with unpacking boys.
Up by the trestle I heard someone say:
"Then they haven't heard of it." I strained to hear their
Quiet funny voices, but it turned to day.

What do the students talk about all day?
Today the dean said: "There's a new boy lost."
He said it to the matron, I could hear their
Footsteps in the corridor, but it was empty.
I must tell them what I heard those people say.
When I get up I'll tell the other boys.

I liked home better, I don't like these boys.
When I wake up I think: "It's dark today."

When I go out these people hardly say
A word to me, I wrote home I had lost
My fountain pen, my mail-box is still empty
Because they've all forgotten me, they love their

New friends better—if I don't get their
Letters ever I don't care, I like these boys
Better than them, I'll write them. "We've still one room
    empty,"
The matron told the man who came today.
How *could* she lie like that? When the roads leave here
    they're lost,
The signs in the country can't think of what to say.

Someone must know. The people here all say
"I don't," I dream I ask them, and I see their
Thoughts don't either, all of them are lost.
Don't signs, don't roads know any more than boys?
When I feel better, they'll wake up one day
And find *my* bed's the one that's empty.

LOSS

Bird of the spray, the tree of bones:
The tendrils shower you with dew, the smells
Of petals patter to the holes of bone—
The yellow nostrils feathered with a bar
That stripes, like blood, your ragged wings;
But the harsh, stopped sounds, the iron of your life,
Rust in the rains of autumn; and the drifts
Entomb, at last, the small nest where a skull
Flimsier than an egg, a drumstick like a straw
Lie like the crushed works of a watch: your child. . . .
When the roofs rise to you, and last year's limb
Holds a cone to your bill, and you hang hammering,
Does the down pulse still, an aching ball,
In your sleek, beaked, uncertain skull?

THE BREATH OF NIGHT

The moon rises. The red cubs rolling
In the ferns by the rotten oak
Stare over a marsh and a meadow
To the farm's white wisp of smoke.

A spark burns, high in heaven.
Deer thread the blossoming rows
Of the old orchard, rabbits
Hop by the well-curb. The cock crows

From the tree by the widow's walk;
Two stars, in the trees to the west,
Are snared, and an owl's soft cry
Runs like a breath through the forest.

Here too, though death is hushed, though joy
Obscures, like night, their wars,
The beings of this world are swept
By the Strife that moves the stars.

AFTERWARDS

(*Four adaptations from Corbière's* RONDELS POUR APRÈS)

I

Sleep: here's your bed . . . You'll not come, any more, to
    ours.
The hungry sleep, and are fed?—Your tongue is all grass.
Sleep: oh, they love you, now—the loved one is always
The Other. Dream: the last fields are all flowers.

Sleep: they'll call you star-snatcher, bareback-rider
Of the rays! . . . though it will be dark there, very dark.
And the angel of attics, at dusk—lean spider,
Hope—comes to spin, for your vacant brow, its webs.

Veiled silencer! . . . But for you a kiss is waiting
Under the veil . . . where, no one knows; close your eyes to
    see.
Laugh: here under the pall, the first prize is waiting.

—They'll break your nose with a smart blow of the censer,
A fine bouquet! for the big, blooming, tallowy mug
Of à well-to-do sexton with his candle-snuffer.

II

It's getting dark, little thief of starlight!
There're no nights any longer, there're no days.
Sleep . . . till they come for you, child, some morning—
Those who said: *Never!* Those who said: *Always!*

Do you hear their steps? They are not heavy:
Oh, the light feet!—Love has wings . . .
It's getting dark, little thief of starlight!

Don't you hear them asking? . . . You're not listening.
Sleep: it's light, your load of everlastings.
They're not coming at all, your friends the bears,
To throw bricks at your bottle of fireflies.
It's getting dark, little thief of starlight!

III

Good morning! . . . Go to sleep: your candle-end
Is there where they put it; then they left you.
You're not afraid of being alone, though—
Poor little thing, are you? It's light as day.

You scared of that old maid and her ruler!
Go on! . . . Why, who's got the nerve to wake you?
Good evening! . . . Go to sleep: your candle-end . . .

Is out.—There's not even a janitor:
Only, the north wind, the south wind, will come to weigh
In their great scales, a thread of gossamer.
—*They* drive you out in the cold, those flatfeet!
Good night! . . . Go to sleep: your candle-end . . .

IV

Run away, little comet's-hair-comber!
The wild grass, in the wind, will be your hair;
From your broken eye there will gush out the
Will-o'-the-wisps, prisoners in your weak head.

The grave-flowers they call Love-in-Idleness
Will seed there, to swell your earthy laugh . . .
And Solitary's flowers, forget-me-nots.

Go, little poet: your coffin's a plaything
For the undertaker's-men, a sound-box
For your penitentiary's last siren . . .
They think you're dead—they're so dumb, these grown-ups—
Run away, little comet's-hair-comber!

THE PLACE OF DEATH

"The wreath is plaited wicker: the green varnish
Still traps, in its tarred pits, a race of gnats;
The flowers in the fruit-jar fail—and vanish,
Drying a stem for judgment. The outlandish
Angel fixing a grey granite Bible
With his red granite eyeballs; the red squirrel that squats
In the black walnut with a wormy nut,
Gnawing mechanically: these, the red
And white and blue woodpecker hammering
This light-pole, are enough to wake the dead—"
The living student walking with Spinoza
In his thin freckled hand, has sometimes felt,
Sinking upon a mound; the grassy airs,
The wood and meadow of their comprehension,
Have murmured to him, from the yellowing page,
That all determination is negation—
He has felt the boundaries of being fade,
These long-outmoded, mounded, dewy modes
Lapse to the seeding and inhuman Substance
Whose infinite, unchanging, and eternal thought
Is here extended in a thousand graves.
These shining bodies—vagrant as a flaw
Of the breath that, in the made, dead flower, mourns—
Involved in their essences the little existence
That survives their thought of it; in part denied
But real, and hence perfect, they hunch here,
A realm within a realm, the last contrary
Being of all used, persisting things—
Till the avenging angel sheathe his sword,
Forget that he is guardian, and dream

(His pocked head pillowed on the book of Life)
The flower and the fruit-jar Victory,
And these graves serving an eternal God
That happiness itself, and final liberty
Which (from the delta of the Alp-born Rhine)
The dead Spinoza named necessity. . . .
But the squirrel flames within the flaming wood
That soars above the poor mounds and their sigh:
"The pity that made us was not womanish";
But the gay bird hammers at the dying tree
Whose wires bring to the peoples light and death;
But the mourners gather for the dying gnat—
The dancers sparkling in their mating cloud—
And the sounds of the lens-grinder cease:
The mourners and the mourned are one. Once more
The great wind dances from the ends of Time
To breathe upon these leaves the student drops,
Napping an hour on this grassy grave.
But the angel whispers from the leafy tomb,
He is not here—see, see, he is not here;
But the leaves blow home to that inhuman kind
Who play their lives out in the place of death
And—dying, dying—from the unmourned grave
Cry to him: "Only man is miserable."

SELECTED

POEMS

II

BOMBERS

EIGHTH AIR FORCE

If, in an odd angle of the hutment,
A puppy laps the water from a can
Of flowers, and the drunk sergeant shaving
Whistles *O Paradiso!*—shall I say that man
Is not as men have said: a wolf to man?

The other murderers troop in yawning;
Three of them play Pitch, one sleeps, and one
Lies counting missions, lies there sweating
Till even his heart beats: One; One; One.
O murderers! . . . Still, this is how it's done:

This is a war. . . . But since these play, before they die,
Like puppies with their puppy; since, a man,
I did as these have done, but did not die—
I will content the people as I can
And give up these to them: Behold the man!

I have suffered, in a dream, because of him,
Many things; for this last saviour, man,
I have lied as I lie now. But what is lying?
Men wash their hands, in blood, as best they can:
I find no fault in this just man.

THE DEATH OF THE BALL
TURRET GUNNER

From my mother's sleep I fell into the State,
And I hunched in its belly till my wet fur froze.
Six miles from earth, loosed from its dream of life,
I woke to black flak and the nightmare fighters.
When I died they washed me out of the turret with a hose.

LOSSES

It was not dying: everybody died.
It was not dying: we had died before
In the routine crashes—and our fields
Called up the papers, wrote home to our folks,
And the rates rose, all because of us.
We died on the wrong page of the almanac,
Scattered on mountains fifty miles away;
Diving on haystacks, fighting with a friend,
We blazed up on the lines we never saw.
We died like aunts or pets or foreigners.
(When we left high school nothing else had died
For us to figure we had died like.)

In our new planes, with our new crews, we bombed
The ranges by the desert or the shore,
Fired at towed targets, waited for our scores—
And turned into replacements and woke up
One morning, over England, operational.
It wasn't different: but if we died
It was not an accident but a mistake
(But an easy one for anyone to make).
We read our mail and counted up our missions—
In bombers named for girls, we burned
The cities we had learned about in school—
Till our lives wore out; our bodies lay among
The people we had killed and never seen.
When we lasted long enough they gave us medals;
When we died they said, "Our casualties were low."

They said, "Here are the maps"; we burned the cities.

It was not dying—no, not ever dying;
But the night I died I dreamed that I was dead,
And the cities said to me: "Why are you dying?
We are satisfied, if you are; but why did I die?"

TRANSIENT BARRACKS

(1944)

Summer. Sunset. Someone is playing
The ocarina in the latrine:
You Are My Sunshine. A man shaving
Sees—past the day-room, past the night K.P.'s
Bent over a G.I. can of beets
In the yard of the mess—the red and green
Lights of a runway full of '24's.
The first night flight goes over with a roar
And disappears, a star, among mountains.

The day-room radio, switched on next door,
Says, "The thing about you is, you're *real*."
The man sees his own face, black against lather,
In the steamed, starred mirror: it is real.
And the others—the boy in underwear
Hunting for something in his barracks-bags
With a money-belt around his middle—
The voice from the doorway: "Where's the C.Q.?"
"Who wants to know?" "He's gone to the movies."
"Tell him Red wants him to sign his clearance"—
These are. Are what? Are.

                            "Jesus Christ, what a field!"
A gunner without a pass keeps saying
To a gunner without a pass. The man
Puts down his razor, leans to the window,
And looks out into the pattern of the field,
Of light and of darkness. His throat tightens,
His lips stretch into a blinded smile.

He thinks, *The times I've dreamed that I was back* . . .
The hairs on the back of his neck stand up straight.

He only yawns, and finishes shaving.
When the gunner asks him, "When you leaving?"
He says: "I just got in. This is my field."
And thinks: *I'm back for good. The States, the States!*
He puts out his hand to touch it—
And the thing about it is, it's *real.*

SIEGFRIED

In the turret's great glass dome, the apparition, death,
Framed in the glass of the gunsight, a fighter's blinking wing,
Flares softly, a vacant fire. If the flak's inked blurs—
Distributed, statistical—the bombs' lost patterning
Are death, they are death under glass, a chance
For someone yesterday, someone tomorrow; and the fire
That streams from the fighter which is there, not there,
Does not warm you, has not burned them, though they die.
Under the leather and fur and wire, in the gunner's skull,
It is a dream: and he, the watcher, guiltily
Watches the him, the actor, who is innocent.
It happens as it does because it does.
It is unnecessary to understand; if you are still
In this year of our warfare, indispensable
In general, and in particular dispensable
As a cartridge, a life—it is only to enter
So many knots in a window, so many feet;
To switch on for an instant the steel that understands.
Do as they said; as they said, there is always a reason—
Though neither for you nor for the fatal
Knower of wind, speed, pressure: the unvalued facts.
(In Nature there is neither right nor left nor wrong.)

So the bombs fell: through clouds to the island,
The dragon of maps; and the island's fighters
Rose from its ruins, through blind smoke, to the flights—
And fluttered smashed from the machinery of death.
Yet inside the infallible invulnerable
Machines, the skin of steel, glass, cartridges,
Duties, responsibilities, and—surely—deaths,

There was only you; the ignorant life
That grew its weariness and loneliness and wishes
Into your whole wish: "Let it be the way it was.
Let me not matter, let nothing I do matter
To anybody, anybody. Let me be what I was."

And you are home, for good now, almost as you wished;
If you matter, it is as little, almost, as you wished.
If it has changed, still, you have had your wish
And are lucky, as you figured luck—are, truly, lucky.
If it is different, if you are different,
It is not from the lives or the cities;
The world's war, just or unjust—the world's peace, war or
    peace;
But from a separate war: the shell with your name
In the bursting turret, the crystals of your blood
On the splints' wrapped steel, the hours wearing
The quiet body back to its base, its missions done;
And the slow flesh failing, the terrible flesh
Sloughed off at last—and waking, your leg gone,
To the dream, the old, old dream: *it happens,*
It happens as it does, it does, it does—

But not because of you, write the knives of the surgeon,
The gauze of the theatre, the bearded and aging face
In the magic glass; if you wake and understand,
There is always the nurse, the leg, the drug—
If you understand, there is sleep, there is sleep . . .
Reading of victories and sales and nations
Under the changed maps, in the sunlit papers;
Stumbling to the toilet on one clever leg
Of leather, wire, and willow; staring
Past the lawn and the trees to nothing, to the eyes

You looked away from as they looked away: the world out-
    side
You are released to, rehabilitated
—*What will you do now? I don't know*—
It is these. If, standing irresolute
By the whitewashed courthouse, in the leafy street,
You look at the people who look back at you, at home,
And it is different, different—you have understood
Your world at last: you have tasted your own blood.

THE CARRIERS

A PILOT FROM THE CARRIER

Strapped at the center of the blazing wheel,
His flesh ice-white against the shattered mask,
He tears at the easy clasp, his sobbing breaths
Misting the fresh blood lightening to flame,
Darkening to smoke; trapped there in pain
And fire and breathlessness, he struggles free
Into the sunlight of the upper sky—
And falls, a quiet bundle in the sky,
The miles to warmth, to air, to waking:
To the great flowering of his life, the hemisphere
That holds his dangling years. In its long slow sway
The world steadies and is almost still. . . .
He is alone; and hangs in knowledge
Slight, separate, estranged: a lonely eye
Reading a child's first scrawl, the carrier's wake—
The travelling milk-like circle of a miss
Beside the plant-like genius of the smoke
That shades, on the little deck, the little blaze
Toy-like as the glitter of the wing-guns,
Shining as the fragile sun-marked plane
That grows to him, rubbed silver tipped with flame.

PILOTS, MAN YOUR PLANES

Dawn; and the jew's-harp's sawing seesaw song
Plucks at the starlight where the planes are folded
At the lee of their blank, wind-whipped, hunting road—
A road in air, the road to nowhere
Turreted and bucketed with guns, long undermined
With the thousand necessary deaths that breathe
Like fire beside a thousand men, who sleep
Hunched in the punk of Death: slow, dreaming sparks
Who burrow through the block-long, light-split gloom
Of their great hangar underground and oversea
Into the great tanks, dark forever; past the steam
Of turbines, laundries—under rockets,
Bakeries, war-heads, the steel watch-like fish,
To the hull's last plates and atmosphere:
The sea sways with the dazed, blind, groping sway
Of the raw soul drugged with sleep, the chancy life
Troubling with dreams its wars, its own earned sea
That stretches year on year, death after death,
And hemisphere on blind black hemisphere
Into the stubborn corners of its earth.

Here in the poor, bleak, guessing haze of dawn
The giant's jew's-harp screeches its two notes
Over and over, over and over; from the roar
Of the fighters waved into the blazing clouds
The lookout lifts his scrubbed tetanic stare
Into the East of light, the empty day.
But on the tubes the raiders oscillate
A mile in every nine or thirteen seconds

To the target's first premonitory bursts;
To the boy with a ball of coffee in his stomach,
Snapping the great light buckles on his groin,
Shifting his raft's hot-water-bottle weight
As he breasts the currents of the bellowing deck
And, locked at last into the bubble, Hope,
Is borne along the foaming windy road
To the air where he alone is still
Above the world's cold, absent, searching roll.

The carrier meshed in its white whirling wake,
The gray ship sparkling from the blue-black sea,
The little carrier—erupts in flak,
One hammering, hysterical, tremendous fire.
Flickering through flashes, the stained rolling clouds,
The air jarred like water tilted in a bowl,
The red wriggling tracers—colonies
Whose instant life annexes the whole sky—
Hunt out the one end they have being for,
Are metamorphosed into one pure smear
Of flame, and die
In the maniacal convulsive spin
Of the raider with a wing snapped off, the plane
Trailing its flaming kite's-tail to the wave.
A miss's near, near bloom, a hill of foam,
Is bulged skyward, crashes back; crest after crest
Patterns the ships' cat's-cradle wakes, the racing
Swells that hiss outward from a plane's quenched flame:
There is traced in the thousand meetings of the grave
Of matter and of matter, man and man,
The print of the running feet upon the waves. . . .
The Jill threads her long, blind, unbearable

Way into fire (the waves lick past her, her whole sky
Is tracer and the dirt of flak, the fire
Flung from the muzzles riddling sea and sky),
Comes on, comes on, comes on; and the fighter flames to her
Through his own flak, the hammering guns
Stitch one long line along his wing, his gear
Falls, his dive staggers as his tracer strikes,
And he breaks off and somersaults into the sea.
Under the canopy's dark strangling green,
The darkening canopy, he struggles free
To float into the choking white, to breathe—
His huge leg floating and immovable,
His goggles blackened with his own bright blood—
On the yellow raft, to see his carrier
Still firing, but itself a fire, its planes
Flung up like matches from the stern's white burst.
Now rockets arch above the deck's great blaze,
Shells break from it, trail after trail; its steel
Melts in steam into the sea, its tanks explode
In one last overwhelming sound; and silently
The ship, a flame, sinks home into the sea.
The pilot holds his striped head patiently
Up out of the dancing smother of the sea
And weeps with hatred, longing, agony—
The sea rises and settles; and the ship is gone.

The planes fly off looking for a carrier,
Destroyers curve in their long hunting arcs
Through the dead of the carrier: the dazed, vomiting,
Oil-blackened and fire-blistered, saved or dying men
Cling with cramped shaking fingers to the lines
Lowered from their old life: the pilot,

Drugged in a blanket, straining up to gulp
From the mug that scrapes like chalk against his mouth,
Knows, knows at last; he yawns the chattering yawn
Of effort and anguish, of hurt hating helplessness—
Yawns sobbingly, his head falls back, he sleeps.

THE DEAD WINGMAN

Seen on the sea, no sign; no sign, no sign
In the black firs and terraces of hills
Ragged in mist. The cone narrows, snow
Glares from the bleak walls of a crater. No.
Again the houses jerk like paper, turn,
And the surf streams by: a port of toys
Is starred with its fires and faces; but no sign.

In the level light, over the fiery shores,
The plane circles stubbornly: the eyes distending
With hatred and misery and longing, stare
Over the blackening ocean for a corpse.
The fires are guttering; the dials fall,
A long dry shudder climbs along his spine,
His fingers tremble; but his hard unchanging stare
Moves unacceptingly: *I have a friend*.

The fires are grey; no star, no sign
Winks from the breathing darkness of the carrier
Where the pilot circles for his wingman; where,
Gliding above the cities' shells, a stubborn eye
Among the embers of the nations, achingly
Tracing the circles of that worn, unchanging *No*—
The lives' long war, lost war—the pilot sleeps.

BURNING THE LETTERS

(*The wife of a pilot killed in the Pacific is speaking several years after his death. She was once a Christian, a Protestant.*)

Here in my head, the home that is left for you,
You have not changed; the flames rise from the sea
And the sea changes: the carrier, torn in two,
Sinks to its planes—the corpses of the carrier
Are strewn like ashes on the star-reflecting sea;
Are gathered, sewn with weights, are sunk.
The gatherers disperse.
                    Here to my hands
From the sea's dark, incalculable calm,
The unchanging circle of the universe,
The letters float: the set yellowing face
Looks home to me, a child's at last,
From the cut-out paper; and the licked
Lips part in their last questioning smile.
The poor labored answers, still unanswering;
The faded questions—questioning so much,
I thought then—questioning so little;
Grew younger, younger, as my eyes grew old,
As that dreamed-out and wept-for wife,
Your last unchanging country, changed
Out of your own rejecting life—a part
Of accusation and of loss, a child's eternally—
Into my troubled separate being.

A child has her own faith, a child's.
In its savage figures—worn down, now, to death—
Men's one life issues, neither out of earth

Nor from the sea, the last dissolving sea,
But out of death: by man came death
And his Life wells from death, the death of Man.
The hunting flesh, the broken blood
Glimmer within the tombs of earth, the food
Of the lives that burrow under the hunting wings
Of the light, of the darkness: dancing, dancing,
The flames grasp flesh with their last searching grace—
Grasp as the lives have grasped: the hunted
Pull down the hunter for his unused life
Parted into the blood, the dark, veined bread
Later than all law. The child shudders, aging:
The peering savior, stooping to her clutch,
His talons cramped with his own bartered flesh,
Pales, flickers, and flares out. In the darkness—darker
With the haunting after-images of light—
The dying God, the eaten Life
Are the nightmare I awaken from to night.

(The flames dance over life. The mourning slaves
In their dark secrecy, come burying
The slave bound in another's flesh, the slave
Freed once, forever, by another's flesh:
The Light flames, flushing the passive face
With its eternal life.)
                              The lives are fed
Into the darkness of their victory;
The ships sink, forgotten; and the sea
Blazes to darkness: the unsearchable
Death of the lives lies dark upon the life
That, bought by death, the loved and tortured lives,
Stares westward, passive, to the blackening sea.
In the tables of the dead, in the unopened almanac,

The head, charred, featureless—the unknown mean—
Is thrust from the waters like a flame, is torn
From its last being with the bestial cry
Of its pure agony. O death of all my life,
Because of you, because of you, I have not died,
By your death I have lived.

                      The sea is empty.
As I am empty, stirring the charred and answered
Questions about your home, your wife, your cat
That stayed at home with me—that died at home
Gray with the years that gleam above you there
In the great green grave where you are young
And unaccepting still. Bound in your death,
I choose between myself and you, between your life
And my own life: it is finished.

                      Here in my head
There is room for your black body in its shroud,
The dog-tags welded to your breastbone, and the flame
That winds above your death and my own life
And the world of my life. The letters and the face
That stir still, sometimes, with your fiery breath—
Take them, O grave! Great grave of all my years,
The unliving universe in which all life is lost,
Make yours the memory of that accepting
And accepted life whose fragments I cast here.

PRISONERS

STALAG LUFT

In the yard, by the house of boxes,
I lay in the ditch with my bow;
And the train's long mourning whistle
Wailed from the valley below
Till the sound of my rabbit gnawing
Was the grasses' tickling shadow,
And I lay dazed in my halo
Of sunlight, a napping echo.

I saw through rainbow lashes
The barred and melting gaze
Of my far-raiding captors.
(The dappled mustangs graze
By the quills of the milky leggings.)
After some feverish days
They smile, and the numbing laces
Are cut from my wrists with praise.

When I woke the rabbit was gnawing
His great, slow, ragged bites
From the wood of the wired-in hutches,
And dusk had greyed the white
Leghorns hunched on the roosts of their run.
The train mourned below
For the captives—a thinning echo. . . .
It all comes back to me now.

JEWS AT HAIFA

The freighter, gay with rust,
Coasts to a bare wharf of the harbor.
From the funnel's shade (the arbor
Of gourds from which the prophet, without trust,
Watched his old enemies,
The beings of this earth) I scrutinize

The hundreds at the rail
Lapped in the blue blaze of this sea
Who stare till their looks fail
At the earth that they are promised; silently
See the sand-bagged machine-guns,
The red-kneed soldiers blinking in the sun.

A machine-gun away
Are men with our faces: we are torn
With the live blaze of day—
Till we feel shifting, wrenched apart, the worn
Named stones of our last knowledge:
That all men wish our death. Here on the edge

Of the graves of Europe
We believe: truly, we are not dead;
It seems to us that hope
Is possible—that even mercy is permitted
To men on this earth,
To Jews on this earth. . . . But at Cyprus, the red earth,

The huts, the trembling wire
That wreathes us, are to us familiar

As death. All night, the fires
Float their sparks up to the yellow stars;
From the steel, stilted tower
The light sweeps over us. We whisper: "Ours."

Ours; and the stones slide home.
There is no hope; "in all this world
There is no other wisdom
Than ours: we have understood the world,"
We think; but hope, in dread
Search for one doubt, and whisper: "Truly, we are not dead."

PRISONERS

Within the wires of the post, unloading the cans of garbage,
The three in soiled blue denim (the white *P* on their backs
Sending its chilly *North* six yards to the turning blackened
Sights of the cradled rifle, to the eyes of the yawning guard)
Go on all day being punished, go on all month, all year
Loading, unloading; give their child's, beast's sigh—of despair,
Of endurance and of existence; look unexpectingly
At the big guard, dark in his khaki, at the dust of the blazing
   plain,
At the running or crawling soldiers in their soiled and shape-
   less green.

The prisoners, the guards, the soldiers—they are all, in their
   way, being trained.
From these moments, repeated forever, our own new world
   will be made.

O MY NAME IT IS SAM HALL

Three prisoners—the biggest black—
    And their one guard stand
By the new bridge over the drainage ditch:
    They listen once more to the band

Whose marches crackle each day at this hour
    From the speakers of the post.
The planes drone over; the clouds of summer
    Blow by and are lost

In the air that they and the crews have conquered—
    But the prisoners still stand
Listening a little after the marches.
    Then they trudge through the sand

To the straggling grass, and the castor bushes,
    And the whitewashed rocks
That stand to them for an army and Order
    (Though their sticks and sacks

And burned slack faces and ambling walk—
    The guard's gleaming yawn—
Are as different as if the four were fighting
    A war of their own).

They graze a while for scraps; one is whistling.
    When the guard begins
Sam Hall in his slow mountain voice
    They all stop and grin.

A CAMP IN THE PRUSSIAN FOREST

I walk beside the prisoners to the road.
Load on puffed load,
Their corpses, stacked like sodden wood,
Lie barred or galled with blood

By the charred warehouse. No one comes today
In the old way
To knock the fillings from their teeth;
The dark, coned, common wreath

Is plaited for their grave—a kind of grief.
The living leaf
Clings to the planted profitable
Pine if it is able;

The boughs sigh, mile on green, calm, breathing mile,
From this dead file
The planners ruled for them. . . . One year
They sent a million here:

Here men were drunk like water, burnt like wood.
The fat of good
And evil, the breast's star of hope
Were rendered into soap.

I paint the star I sawed from yellow pine—
And plant the sign
In soil that does not yet refuse
Its usual Jews

Their first asylum. But the white, dwarfed star—
This dead white star—
Hides nothing, pays for nothing; smoke
Fouls it, a yellow joke,

The needles of the wreath are chalked with ash,
A filmy trash
Litters the black woods with the death
Of men; and one last breath

Curls from the monstrous chimney. . . . I laugh aloud
Again and again;
The star laughs from its rotting shroud
Of flesh. O star of men!

CAMPS AND FIELDS

A LULLABY

For wars his life and half a world away
The soldier sells his family and days.
He learns to fight for freedom and the State;
He sleeps with seven men within six feet.

He picks up matches and he cleans out plates;
Is lied to like a child, cursed like a beast.
They crop his head, his dog tags ring like sheep
As his stiff limbs shift wearily to sleep.

Recalled in dreams or letters, else forgot,
His life is smothered like a grave, with dirt;
And his dull torment mottles like a fly's
The lying amber of the histories.

MAIL CALL

The letters always just evade the hand.
One skates like a stone into a beam, falls like a bird.
Surely the past from which the letters rise
Is waiting in the future, past the graves?
The soldiers are all haunted by their lives.

Their claims upon their kind are paid in paper
That establishes a presence, like a smell.
In letters and in dreams they see the world.
They are waiting: and the years contract
To an empty hand, to one unuttered sound—

The soldier simply wishes for his name.

ABSENT WITH OFFICIAL LEAVE

The lights are beginning to go out in the barracks.
They persist or return, as the wakeful hollow,
But only for a moment; then the windows blacken
For all the hours of the soldier's life.

It is life into which he composes his body.
He covers his ears with his pillow, and begins to drift
(Like the plumes the barracks trail into the sky)
Past the laughs, the quarrels, and the breath of others

To the ignorant countries where civilians die
Inefficiently, in their spare time, for nothing . . .
The curved roads hopping through the aimless green
Dismay him, and the cottages where people cry

For themselves and, sometimes, for the absent soldier—
Who inches through hedges where the hunters sprawl
For birds, for birds; who turns in ecstasy
Before the slow small fires the women light

His charmed limbs, all endearing from the tub.
He dozes, and the washed locks trail like flax
Down the dark face; the unaccusing eyes
That even the dream's eyes are averted from

See the wind puff down the chimney, warm the hands
White with the blossoms it pretends are snow . . .
He moans like a bear in his enchanted sleep,
And the grave mysterious beings of his years—

The causes who mourn above his agony like trees—
Are moved for their child, and bend across his limbs
The one face opening for his life, the eyes
That look without shame even into his.

And the man awakes, and sees around his life
The night that is never silent, broken with the sighs
And patient breathing of the dark companions
With whom he labors, sleeps, and dies.

A FRONT

Fog over the base: the beams ranging
From the five towers pull home from the night
The crews cold in fur, the bombers banging
Like lost trucks down the levels of the ice.
A glow drifts in like mist (how many tons of it?),
Bounces to a roll, turns suddenly to steel
And tires and turrets, huge in the trembling light.
The next is high, and pulls up with a wail,
Comes round again—no use. And no use for the rest
In drifting circles out along the range;
Holding no longer, changed to a kinder course,
The flights drone southward through the steady rain.
The base is closed. . . . But one voice keeps on calling,
The lowering pattern of the engines grows;
The roar gropes downward in its shaky orbit
For the lives the season quenches. Here below
They beg, order, are not heard; and hear the darker
Voice rising: *Can't you hear me? Over. Over—*
All the air quivers, and the east sky glows.

THE SICK NOUGHT

Do the wife and baby travelling to see
Your grey pajamas and sick worried face
Remind you of something, soldier? I remember
You convalescing washing plates, or mopping
The endless corridors your shoes had scuffed;
And in the crowded room you rubbed your cheek
Against your wife's thin elbow like a pony.
But you are something.there are millions of.
How can I care about you much, or pick you out
From all the others other people loved
And sent away to die for them? You are a ticket
Someone bought and lost on, a stray animal:
You have lost even the right to be condemned.
I see you looking helplessly around, in histories,
Bewildered with your terrible companions, Pain
And Death and Empire: what have you understood, to die?
Were you worth, soldiers, all that people said
To be spent so willingly? Surely your one theory, to live,
Is nonsense to the practice of the centuries.
What is demanded in the trade of states
But lives, your lives?—the one commodity.

LEAVE

One winds through firs—their weeds are ferns
Four brown feet high—to aspens three feet wide.
Woodpeckers hammer at the pine-cones, upside-down—
The burros wander through the forest with their bells,
And the deer trample the last stalky meadow.
But the plants evolve into a rock, the precipice
Habitual, in Chinese ink, to such a scene;
Persisting in a cleft, one streaming fir
Must shelter at its root a fat philosopher
Reducing to his silence this grey upper world.

But he is missing (dead perhaps, perhaps a prisoner).
Cold, airy, silent, the half-sunken floes
Stream south from the mountain-top: the seven ranges.
Below are the fields, the dim fields—and the fighter
Turning to them with its thin spectral whine;
Below the moss tracks, rock to rock, the fall of water—
The mote dances in a Nature full of squirrels.

THE RANGE IN THE DESERT

Where the lizard ran to its little prey
And a man on a horse rode by in a day
They set their hangars: a continent
Taught its conscripts its unloved intent
In the scrawled fire, the singing lead—
Protocols of the quick and dead.
The wounded gunner, his missions done,
Fired absently in the range's sun;
And, chained with cartridges, the clerk
Sat sweating at his war-time work.
The cold flights bombed—again, again—
The craters of the lunar plain. . . .

All this was priceless: men were paid
For these rehearsals of the raids
That used up cities at a rate
That left the coals without a State
To call another's; till the worse
Ceded at last, without remorse,
Their conquests to their conquerors.
The equations were without two powers.

Profits and death grow marginal:
Only the mourning and the mourned recall
The wars we lose, the wars we win;
And the world is—what it has been.

The lizard's tongue licks angrily
The shattered membranes of the fly.

SECOND AIR FORCE

Far off, above the plain the summer dries,
The great loops of the hangars sway like hills.
Buses and weariness and loss, the nodding soldiers
Are wire, the bare frame building, and a pass
To what was hers; her head hides his square patch
And she thinks heavily: My son is grown.
She sees a world: sand roads, tar-paper barracks,
The bubbling asphalt of the runways, sage,
The dunes rising to the interminable ranges,
The dim flights moving over clouds like clouds.
The armorers in their patched faded green,
Sweat-stiffened, banded with brass cartridges,
Walk to the line; their Fortresses, all tail,
Stand wrong and flimsy on their skinny legs,
And the crews climb to them clumsily as bears.
The head withdraws into its hatch (a boy's),
The engines rise to their blind laboring roar,
And the green, made beasts run home to air.
Now in each aspect death is pure.
(At twilight they wink over men like stars
And hour by hour, through the night, some see
The great lights floating in—from Mars, from Mars.)
How emptily the watchers see them gone.

They go, there is silence; the woman and her son
Stand in the forest of the shadows, and the light
Washes them like water. In the long-sunken city
Of evening, the sunlight stills like sleep
The faint wonder of the drowned; in the evening,
In the last dreaming light, so fresh, so old,

The soldiers pass like beasts, unquestioning,
And the watcher for an instant understands
What there is then no need to understand;
But she wakes from her knowledge, and her stare,
A shadow now, moves emptily among
The shadows learning in their shadowy fields
The empty missions.
                              Remembering,
She hears the bomber calling, *Little Friend!*
To the fighter hanging in the hostile sky,
And sees the ragged flame eat, rib by rib,
Along the metal of the wing into her heart:
The lives stream out, blossom, and float steadily
To the flames of the earth, the flames
That burn like stars above the lands of men.

She saves from the twilight that takes everything
A squadron shipping, in its last parade—
Its dogs run by it, barking at the band—
A gunner walking to his barracks, half-asleep,
Starting at something, stumbling (above, invisible,
The crews in the steady winter of the sky
Tremble in their wired fur); and feels for them
The love of life for life. The hopeful cells
Heavy with someone else's death, cold carriers
Of someone else's victory, grope past their lives
Into her own bewilderment: The years meant *this?*

But for them the bombers answer everything.

THE TRADES

THE RISING SUN

The card-house over the fault
Was spilt in a dream; your mother's terraces
Of hair fell home to hide
The wooden pillow, the sleek dazzled head
That bobbed there, a five-colored cloud.
Above black pines, the last cloud-girdled peak
Was brushed on the starlight like a cone of rice.
The clear flame wavered in the brazier;
The floor, cold under the quilt,
Pressed its cramped ground into your dream.
The great carp, a kite, swam up to you
Along his line; but you were riding there,
A sun in air, the pure sky gazing down
From its six-cornered roof upon the world.
The kettle gave its hissing laugh, you bowed,
The characters of moonlight were your name
Across the bare, old order of the room,
And you awoke. In your rice-marshed, sea-margined plain
The flakes, like petals, blew from peak to peak;
The petals blew from peak to peak, like snow.

Dwarfed and potted cherry, warped
With the sea-wind, frost with moonlight: child,
The hunting ghosts throng here for love
Where water falls, a steady wish;
The *ronin* stalk by, girded with two swords—
These kill, these kill, and have not died;
You raise, as you have raised, the wooden sword—
The great two-handed sword; and your fat breast
Glows, trembling, in the patched
And patchwork armor of your school. . . .
On this stage even a wall is silk
And quakes according to a will; heads roll
From the gutted, kneeling sons by rule.

So man is pressed into obedience
Till even the eldest, unaccounting wish
Of his bull's heart, is safe by rote
From his tormentors—who are honorable
In their way: which is your way, child.

The brushed ink of clerks, the abacus
That tells another's fortune, life by life;
The rice-ball garnished with a shred of flesh
Or plum, or blossom, and thus named—
Are these the commerce of the warrior
Who bowed in blue, a child of four,
To the fathers and their father, Strife?

But War delivers all things—men from men
Into the hope of death: Deliverer,
Who whirled the child's grey ashes from the West
Into the shrine beside the rocks: O Way
That led the twitching body to the flame,

Bring to this temple of the blind, burnt dead
The mourning who awaken from your dream
Before a lacquered box, and take the last
Dry puff of smoke, in memory
Of this weak ghost.

NEW GEORGIA

Sometimes as I woke, the branches beside the stars
Were to me, as I drowsed, the bars of my cell;
The creepers lumped through my blanket, hard as a bed
In the old ward, in the time before the war—

In the days when, supperless, I moaned in sleep
With the stripes of beating, the old, hard, hampering dream
That lay like the chains on my limbs; till I woke
To a world and a year that used me, when I had learned to
    obey.

By the piece with the notch on the stock, by the knife from
    the States,
The tags' chain stirs with the wind; and I sleep
Paid, dead, and a soldier. Who fights for his own life
Loses, loses: I have killed for my world, and am free.

THE SUBWAY FROM
NEW BRITAIN TO THE BRONX

Under the orchid, blooming as it bloomed
In the first black air: in the incessant
Lightning of the trains, tiled swarming tubes
Under the stone and Reason of the states;

Under the orchid flowering from the hot
Dreams of the car-cards, from the black desires
Coiled like converters in the bowels of trade
To break to sunlight in one blinding flame
Of Reason, under the shaking creepers of the isles;

Under the orchid, rank memorial,
From the armature about which crystallized
A life—its tanks, its customers, its Christ—
The rain-forest's tepid siftings leach
Its one solution: of lust, torment, punishment—
Of a man, a man.

              Here under the orchid
Of florists, Geography, and flesh,
A little water and a little dirt
Are forever urban, temperate: a West
Dead in the staring Orient of earth.

The air-fed orchid, the unquestioning
Trades of the leaf, of longing, of the isles
Sigh for you, sparrow, the same yearning sigh
Their beasts gave once, in summer, to the bars
And peoples of the Bronx, their conquerors.

1945: THE DEATH
OF THE GODS

In peace tomorrow, when your slack hands weigh
Upon the causes; when the ores are rust
And the oil laked under the mandates
Has puffed from the turbines; when the ash of life
Is earth that has forgotten the first human sun
Your wisdom found: O bringers of the fire,
When you have shipped our bones home from the bases
To those who think of us, not as we were
(Defiled, annihilated—the forgotten vessels
Of the wrath that formed us; of the murderous
Dull will that worked out its commandment, death
For the disobedient and for us, obedient)—
When you have seen grief wither, death forgotten,
And dread and love, the witnesses of men,
Swallowed up in victory: you who determine
Men's last obedience, yourselves determined
In the first unjudged obedience of greed
And senseless power: you eternal States
Beneath whose shadows men have found the stars
And graves of men: O warring Deities,
Tomorrow when the rockets rise like stars
And earth is blazing with a thousand suns
That set up there within your realms a realm
Whose laws are ecumenical, whose life
Exacts from men a prior obedience—
Must you learn from your makers how to die?

A WARD IN THE STATES

The ward is barred with moonlight,
    The owl hoots from the snowy park.
The wind of the rimed, bare branches
    Slips coldly into the dark

Warmed ward where the muttering soldiers
    Toss, dreaming that they still sigh
For home, for home; that the islands
    Are stretched interminably

Past their lives—past their one wish, murmured
    In the endless, breathless calm
By the grumbling surf, by the branches
    That creak from the splintered palm.

In bed at home, in the moonlight,
    Ah, one lies warm
With fever, the old sweat darkens
    Under the upflung arm

The tangled head; and the parted
    Lips chatter their old sigh,
A breath of mist in the moonlight
    That beams from the wintry sky.

THE WIDE PROSPECT

—saw The Wide Prospect, and the Asian fen—

Who could have figured, when the harnesses improved
And men pumped kobolds from the coal's young seams
There to the west, on Asia's backward cape—
The interest on that first raw capital?
The hegemony only the corpses have escaped?

When the earth turns, the serfs are eaten by the sheep;
The ploughland frees itself from men with deeds.
The old Adam sells his hours to an alderman
(Who adds them, in Arabic, in his black books);
Men learn it takes nine men to make a pin.

The star-led merchants steer with powder and with steel
Past dragonish waters, to the fabled world
Whose ignorant peoples tear the heart with stone.
Their lashed lines transport to the galleons' holds
New vegetables, tobacco, and the gold—the gold

That cracked our veins with credit, till the indices
Of old commodities were changed as Christ,
Till serf and lord were hammered into States
The lettered princes mortgaged for their lace
To lenders shrewder than Poor Richard, crude as Fate.

What traffickers, the captains! How the merchants war!
Beneath their blood and gilt swim like a shade
Black friars who survey with impartial eyes
The flames where Fathers or the heathen die,
Who bless alike the corpses and the Trade.

180

Here the horseman—steel, and backed with wings,
The salt sails rising from the centuries—
Holds laws: the tables flash like steel
Under the hollows of the high head, whitening
The eyes that watch unseeingly, like coins,

The deaths of the peoples. They are entered in his books;
For them he keeps, as God for Adam, work
And death and wisdom. They are money.
Their lives, enchanted to a thousand forms,
Are piled in holds for Europe; and their bones

Work out their ghostly years, despair, and die.
The mills rise from the sea . . . The mother and the son
Stare past the ponies of the pit, to wheels
Beaten from their iron breath, to shuttles
Threading their gnarled and profitable flesh like bones;

Whirled on pulleys to the knife, drayed to the shuttling tramps,
Through post or mission, the long bolts of their lives
Run out, run out: the flesh lasts to those last isles
Where in mine and compound the man-eaters die
Under the cross of their long-eaten Kin.

All die for all. And the planes rise from the years:
The years when, West or West, the cities burn,
And Europe is the colony of colonies—
When men see men once more the food of Man
And their bare lives His last commodity.

THE DEAD IN MELANESIA

Beside the crater and the tattered palm
The trades, the old trades, sigh their local psalm:
But their man-god in his outrigger,
The boars' tusks curling like a nautilus,
Fell to the schooners cruising here for niggers.
To the Nature here these deaths are fabulous;

And yet this world works, grain by grain, into the graves
Till the poor *ronin* in their tank-sealed caves
Are troubled by its alien genius
That takes uncomprehendingly the kites, the snow—
Their decomposing traces. And the conquerors
Who hid their single talent in Chicago,

Des Moines, Cheyenne, are buried with it here.
The including land, mistaking their success,
Takes the tall strangers to its heart like failures:
Each missionary, with his base and cross,
Sprawls in the blood of an untaken beachhead;
And the isles confuse him with their own black dead.

CHILDREN AND CIVILIANS

THE STATE

When they killed my mother it made me nervous;
I thought to myself, It was *right:*
Of course she was crazy, and how she ate!
And she died, after all, in her way, for the State.
But I minded: how queer it was to stare
At one of them not sitting there.

When they drafted Sister I said all night,
"It's healthier there in the fields";
And I'd think, "Now I'm helping to win the War,"
When the neighbors came in, as they did, with my meals.
And I was, I was; but I was scared
With only one of them sitting there.

When they took my cat for the Army Corps
Of Conservation and Supply,
I thought of him there in the cold with the mice
And I cried, and I cried, and I wanted to die.
They were there, and I saw them, and that is my life.
Now there's nothing. I'm dead, and I want to die.

COME TO THE STONE . . .

The child saw the bombers skate like stones across the fields
As he trudged down the ways the summer strewed
With its reluctant foliage; how many giants
Rose and peered down and vanished, by the road
The ants had littered with their crumbs and dead.

"That man is white and red like my clown doll,"
He says to his mother, who has gone away.
"I didn't cry, I didn't cry."
In the sky the planes are angry like the wind.
The people are punishing the people—why?

He answers easily, his foolish eyes
Brightening at that long simile, the world.
The angels sway above his story like balloons.
A child makes everything—except his death—a child's.
Come to the stone and tell me why I died.

THE ANGELS AT HAMBURG

In caves emptied of their workers, turning
From spent mines to the ruins of factories,
The soul sleeps under the hive of earth.
Freed for an hour from its deadly dreams
Of Good and Evil, from the fiery judge
Who walks like an angel through the guilty state
The world sets up within the laboring breast,
It falls past Heaven into Paradise:
Here man spins his last Eden like a worm.

Here is Knowledge, the bombs tempt fruitlessly.
In the darkness under the fiery missions
That fail, and are renewed by every season,
He is estranged from suffering, and willingly
Floats like a moon above the starving limbs
Oppressed with remembrance, tossed uncertainly
Under the angels' deadly paths—he whispers,
"My punishment is more than I can bear."
He knows neither good, nor evil, nor the angels,
Nor their message: There is no justice, man, but death.
He watches the child and the cat and the soldier dying,
Not loving, not hating their judges, who neither love nor hate;
In his heart Hamburg is no longer a city,
There is no more state.

The judges come to judge man in the night.
How bitterly they look on his desire!
Here at midnight there is no darkness,
At day no light.

The air is smoke and the earth ashes
Where he was fire;
He looks from his grave for life, and judgment
Rides over his city like a star.

PROTOCOLS

(Birkenau, Odessa; the children speak alternately.)

We went there on the train. *They had big barges that they
    towed,*
We stood up, there were so many I was squashed.
There was a smoke-stack, then they made me wash.
It was a factory, I think. *My mother held me up*
And I could see the ship that made the smoke.

When I was tired my mother carried me.
She said, "Don't be afraid." But I was only tired.
Where we went there is no more Odessa.
They had water in a pipe—like rain, but hot;
The water there is deeper than the world

And I was tired and fell in in my sleep
And the water drank me. That is what I think.
And I said to my mother, "Now I'm washed and dried,"
My mother hugged me, and it smelled like hay
And that is how you die. And that is how you die.

THE METAMORPHOSES

Where I spat in the harbor the oranges were bobbing
All salted and sodden, with eyes in their rinds;
The sky was all black where the coffee was burning,
And the rust of the freighters had reddened the tide.

But soon all the chimneys were burning with contracts,
The tankers rode low in the oil-black bay,
The wharves were a maze of the crated bombers,
And they gave me a job and I worked all day.

And the orders are filled; but I float in the harbor,
All tarry and swollen, with gills in my sides,
The sky is all black where the carrier's burning,
And the blood of the transports is red on the tide.

THE TRUTH

When I was four my father went to Scotland.
They *said* he went to Scotland.

When I woke up I think I thought that I was dreaming—
I was so little then that I thought dreams
Are in the room with you, like the cinema.
That's why you don't dream when it's still light—
They pull the shades down when it is, so you can sleep.
I thought that then, but that's not right.
Really it's in your head.

And it was light then—light at *night*.
I heard Stalky bark outside.
But really it was Mother crying—
She coughed so hard she cried.
She kept shaking Sister,
She shook her and shook her.
I thought Sister had had her nightmare.
But he wasn't barking, he had died.
There was dirt all over Sister.
It was all streaks, like mud. I cried.
She didn't, but she was older.
                              I thought she didn't
Because she was older, I thought Stalky had just gone.
I got *everything* wrong.
I didn't get one single thing right.
It seems to me that I'd have thought
It didn't happen, like a dream,
Except that it was light. At night.
They burnt our house down, they burnt down London.

Next day my mother cried all day, and after that
She said to me when she would come to see me:
"Your father has gone away to Scotland.
He will be back after the war."

The war then was different from the war now.
The war now is *nothing*.

I used to live in London till they burnt it.
What was it like? It was just like here.
No, that's the truth.
My mother would come here, some, but she would cry.
She said to Miss Elise, "He's not himself";
She said, "Don't you love me any more at all?"
I was *my*self.
Finally she wouldn't come at all.
She never said one thing my father said, or Sister.
Sometimes she did,
Sometimes she was the same, but that was when I dreamed it.
I could tell I was dreaming, she was just the same.

That Christmas she bought me a toy dog.

I asked her what was its name, and when she didn't know
I asked her over, and when she didn't know
I said, "You're not my mother, you're not my mother.
She *hasn't* gone to Scotland, she is dead!"
And she said, "Yes, he's dead, he's dead!"
And cried and cried; she *was* my mother,
She put her arms around me and we cried.

SOLDIERS

PORT OF EMBARKATION

Freedom, farewell! Or so the soldiers say;
And all the freedoms they spent yesterday
Lure from beyond the graves, a war away.
The cropped skulls resonate the wistful lies
Of dead civilians: truth, reason, justice;
The foolish ages haunt their unaccepting eyes.

From the green gloom of the untroubled seas
Their little bones (the coral of the histories)
Foam into marches, exultation, victories:
Who will believe the blood curled like a moan
From the soaked lips, a century from home—
The slow lives sank from being like a dream?

THE LINES

After the centers' naked files, the basic line
Standing outside a building in the cold
Of the late or early darkness, waiting
For meals or mail or salvage, or to wait
To form a line to form a line to form a line;
After the things have learned that they are things,
Used up as things are, pieces of the plain
Flat object-language of a child or states;
After the lines, through trucks, through transports, to the lines
Where the things die as though they were not things—
But lie as numbers in the crosses' lines;
After the files that ebb into the rows
Of the white beds of the quiet wards, the lines
Where some are salvaged for their state, but some
Remanded, useless, to the centers' files;
After the naked things, told they are men,
Have lined once more for papers, pensions—suddenly
The lines break up, for good; and for a breath,
The longest of their lives, the men are free.

A FIELD HOSPITAL

He stirs, beginning to awake.
A kind of ache
Of knowing troubles his blind warmth; he moans,
And the high hammering drone
Of the first crossing fighters shakes
His sleep to pieces, rakes
The darkness with its skidding bursts, is done.
All that he has known

Floods in upon him; but he dreads
The crooked thread
Of fire upon the darkness: "The great drake
Flutters to the icy lake—
The shotguns stammer in my head.
I lie in my own bed,"
He whispers, "dreaming"; and he thinks to wake.
The old mistake.

A cot creaks; and he hears the groan
He thinks his own—
And groans, and turns his stitched, blind, bandaged head
Up to the tent-flap, red
With dawn. A voice says, "Yes, this one";
His arm stings; then, alone,
He neither knows, remembers—but instead
Sleeps, comforted.

N<small>OW</small> IT IS NO LONGER THE WAR, BUT A war: our own has taken its place. The World War is only the First World War; and, truly, these are photographs not of the world, but of the first world. But for twenty years, while the wire and trenches in the mud were everybody's future, how could any of it seem old-fashioned to us?—it was our death. But when we died differently we saw that it was old.

The men who seize Princip wear little vests and sashes, skirts with under-leggings, fezzes; one tugs at his arm in a stand-up collar, peg-top trousers, and a chauffeur's cap; and he himself has hair like a rope wig, a face the camera draws out into the Mad Hatter's. The Archduke, spotted with the blood that does, indeed, look exactly like our own (the trees, too, are human), has moustaches like a Keystone Cop's. No one is laughing.

This, next week, is the war the crowds hear. The crowds in their stiff straw hats, their starched high collars— the women in shirtwaists or muslin, their hats shapeless with fruit and flowers—the crowds stand in black under the summer sun, holding their rolled-up umbrellas: does Job fear God for naught? It is a universe where even the Accuser is troubled, and Time hesitates: Surely these States are eternal? Troops march through the crowds; some in blue swallow-tailed coats, their bayonets high as hop-poles; some in grey. One of these, his pockets bulging, wears a round cap like an old joke; he is smoking a cigar, and breaks ranks to take the bouquet of a middle-aged woman, who holds the flowers out with her left hand and bows her head so that her face is hidden. Next page an old woman walking along a road, leading a white horse—he is pulling off her home, in a wooden cart half again as high as she—bows her head exactly as far. These are the poor, whom we have with us: in their shoulders there is neither grief nor joy, something more passive than acceptance.

The wet sand is torn by feet, the grass blows by the marsh's edge; here, lost in the flat land, seven soldiers are waiting. They lie looking into the horizon, around the machine-gun they have brought here on a cart; to the cart a dog is harnessed—a spotted medium-sized dog, who stares backward and upward into the eyes of man. *Unorganized Innocence: an impossibility*, said Blake; but this was possible; and it vanishes, leaving only this print, beneath the wave that goose-steps into Brussels. Under the spiked enameled helmets, behind moustaches issued with the cheap field-grey, the faces know better than their game; but their officer, wood in his saddle, holds his sabre out like Ney, and stares forward and downward into the camera's lens.

Now the forts of Antwerp, broken into blocks, slide into a moat as bergs break off into the sea; the blocks, metamorphosed into the dead, sprawl naked as grave-mounds in the stalky fields; black crowds, their faces fiery with evening, stumble through the typed bodies nailed in rows outside a postoffice; the innocent armies, marching over the meadows to three haystacks, a mill-dam, and a hedge, dig a trench for their dead and vanish there. Over them the machine-guns hammer, like presses, the speeches into a common tongue: the object-language of the Old Man of Laputa; here is the fetishism of one commodity, all the values translated into a piece of meat. A wire-coiled Uhlan, pressing to his lips a handkerchief dampened with chlorine, looks timidly into the great blaze of the flame-thrower his supply-sergeant hands to him; the sergeant takes away the haystacks, one by one, the hedge, the mill-dam, and puts in their place the craters of the moon. The winter comes now, flake by flake; the snowflakes or soldiers (it is impossible to distinguish—under the microscope each one is individual) are numbered by accountants, who trace with their fingers, in black trenches filled with the dancing snow, the unlikely figures of the dead. The fingers, wooden with cold, work slowly and at last are still; the last figures, whitening, whitening, vanish into their shining ground . . .

But before, somewhere else, there is a soldier. He is half-sitting, half-lying against what seems a hillside; but at the bottom, under the grass and weeds and dirt, there are sandbags. He is dressed all in grey—even his boots are grey, and merge imperceptibly into his trousers, just as his coat and hat merge imperceptibly into his face—grey with wrinkles and spots and ragged holes: he has become grey as a snowman is white. He has pushed his grey hand between his grey knees (drawn up a little) as if it were cold; but his dark brown hand is folded under his head, as if he were leaning on it patiently or thoughtfully. Part of his face is dark brown, and the rest has trickles of dark brown like contours on its grey; his nose is the white bill of a goose.

He has been dead for months—that is to say for minutes, for a century; if because of his death his armies have conquered the world, and have brought to its peoples food, justice, and art, it has been a good bargain for all of them but him. Underneath his picture there is written, about his life, his death, or his war: *Es war ein Traum.*

It is the dream from which no one wakes.

GUNNER

Did they send me away from my cat and my wife
To a doctor who poked me and counted my teeth,
To a line on a plain, to a stove in a tent?
Did I nod in the flies of the schools?

And the fighters rolled into the tracer like rabbits,
The blood froze over my splints like a scab—
Did I snore, all still and grey in the turret,
Till the palms rose out of the sea with my death?

And the world ends here, in the sand of a grave,
All my wars over? . . . It was easy as that!
Has my wife a pension of so many mice?
Did the medals go home to my cat?

GOOD-BYE, WENDOVER;
GOOD-BYE, MOUNTAIN HOME

(*Wendover, Mountain Home, Lowrie, Kearns, Laredo: Second Air Force fields. Men going to Overseas Replacement Depots like Kearns were called ORD's*).

Wives on day-coaches traveling with a baby
From one room outside Lowrie to a room near Kearns.
Husbands firing into sagebrush near Wendover,
Mesquite outside Laredo: you're on Shipping. Kearns.

Or if it isn't Kearns, it might as well be Kearns.
(I asked the first sergeant up at Operations.
The Wac at Transportation says you're ORD.)
The orders are cut. I tell you you're on Shipping
And you might as well get used to it, you ORD's.

Wives on day-coaches crying, talking to sailors,
Going home, going somewhere from a room near Kearns.
Husbands getting shots for cholera, yellow fever,
And shipping in the morning on a train from Kearns.

Or if it wasn't Kearns, it might as well be Kearns.
(I asked, but they've forgotten. Up at History
There're no wives, no day-coaches, and no ORD.)
The book is finished. I tell you you're not in it
And you might as well get used to it, you ORD's.

THE SURVIVOR AMONG
GRAVES

There are fields beyond. The world there obeys
The living Word; names, numbers do for this.
The grave's cross, the grave's grass, the grave's polished granite
THESE DIED THAT WE MIGHT LIVE
                                    —that I may live!—
Are customary, but not necessary;
This world needs only the dead.
                          That all-replacing dream
Through which our dark lives led in waiting—
The dream I woke to, that holds you sleepers still—
What is it now, The War? A war now, numbered
As your lives and graves are numbered; that one can lose,
That we have lost.
                    Lost too, the overmastering
Demand that delivered us from all demands
Except its metal *Live!*—that left bare life
The sense life made, stripping from all there is
Its old, own sense: till simply to restore
One—to sit reading the papers on a Sunday morning—
Was enough, an end beyond all ends, the dream
Dreams dream of . . . until this, at last restored,
Was an end no longer, and the senselessness
Our lives had reached from came to seem the sense
We had reached to; and we saw that we had lived
For some few years longer than the rest within
The future where, the child says, *we shall live*.

Where shall we live? For your lives are not lived
But, there in mid-air, cease, and do not fall

And are what is not, but that could have been.
And ours are—what they are; and, slowly, end.

Our lives have made their peace with the existence
That has leached from their old essences, in time,
All that is not itself. What we remember
You are: a waiting.
                        Without you, all you dead,
What rag could wipe this scrawled slate clean of life,
What haunted body guess for me the world
Of which this earth, this life, are one spoiled seed?

We endure to fulfillment; it is victory
The living lose. And loss? The living lose
All things alike; and, recompensed, in the survival
That brings them, daily, that indifference, death,
Ride in the triumph of the world in chains—
Their world, their triumph.
                        We sleep lightly; waking,
Some still success, succession, weighs us down,
Enchanting our limbs to yours . . . our veins averted
Into another world, our vacant hope
Long since fulfilled, our last necessity
Remembered sometimes (with the accustomed smile
Of cold acceptance) as the luxury our youth
Demanded ignorantly.
                        Your ignorance
Is immortal in your deaths, a spring
Of blood to which the living come, to bend
In dry half-dreaming supplication . . .

The haunters and the haunted, among graves,
Mirror each other sightlessly; in soundless

Supplication, a last unheard
Unison, reach to each other: *Say again,*
Say the voices, *say again*
That life is—what it is not;
That, somewhere, there is—something, something;
That we are waiting; that we are waiting.

A WAR

There set out, slowly, for a Different World,
At four, on winter mornings, different legs . . .
You can't break eggs without making an omelette
—That's what they tell the eggs.

TERMS

I

One-armed, one-legged, and one-headed,
The pensioner sits in the sun.
He is telling a story to the leaf
Of the new maple in his new yard:
"The Department of the Interior has sent Jack Frost with a
    spray-gun
To paint you red."
The leaf pulls hard
To get away—it believes the man—
And a blue Chevrolet sedan
Draws up and leaves a check for the man in the mail-box.

"You're as good as dead,"
Says the man, with a mocking smile, to the leaf;
And somebody knocks
At the front door, the man doesn't answer,
But sits back in his white board chair—
Holding a mallet, by a stake with rainbow rings—
And rubs his eyes, and yawns like a dog when the dog
Next door whines and rattles its chain.
He looks at the leaf, as he looks at things,
With mixed feelings—
And says, "I've changed."

The good dreams keep haunting
The ghost with a check in the mail-box, the fox
With four quick brown wooden legs.
With one military brush, in the morning,

He pulls forward, or brushes back, the fair
Hair on the living head,
And brushes his firm white teeth, and the porcelain jacket
On his left front tooth, that is dead.
The leaf is alive, and it is going to be dead;
It is like any other leaf.
You keep flipping the coin and it comes down heads
And nobody has ever seen it come down anything but heads
And the man has stopped looking:

it's heads.

He looks at the leaf—it is green—
And says with a flat black leather gesture:
"Never again."

II

He says: "My arm and leg—
My wooden arm, my wooden leg—
Wrestled with each other all last night
The way you whet a carving-knife
Till they stood crisscross against dawn
Over what seemed to me a tomb.
I felt for the dog-tags on the cross.

"I could find one number on the leg
And a different number on the arm.
The grave was empty.

"I thought first, 'I have arisen,'
And looked up past the cross into the dawn
And saw my own head, burning there,

Go out.
        But in the darkness
The leaves fell one by one, like checks,
Into the grave;
And I thought: I am my own grave.

"Then I awoke: I could see the toaster
On its rack over the waffle-iron
And the dew on the wickets; at breakfast the bread
Pops up, all brown, from its—
                        'It's all a dream,'
I said to myself. 'I am a grave dreaming
That it is a living man.' "

The man, as he has learned to,
Gets up and walks to the door.
As he opens the door
He watches his hand opening the door
And holds out his good hand—
And stares at them both, and laughs;
Then he says softly: "I am a man."

THE WOMAN AT
THE WASHINGTON ZOO

POEMS & TRANSLATIONS

RANDALL JARRELL

To Mary

CONTENTS

THE WOMAN
AT THE
WASHINGTON
ZOO

THE WOMAN AT THE WASHINGTON ZOO

The saris go by me from the embassies.

Cloth from the moon. Cloth from another planet.
They look back at the leopard like the leopard.

And I. . . .
                this print of mine, that has kept its color
Alive through so many cleanings; this dull null
Navy I wear to work, and wear from work, and so
To my bed, so to my grave, with no
Complaints, no comment: neither from my chief,
The Deputy Chief Assistant, nor his chief—
Only I complain. . . . this serviceable
Body that no sunlight dyes, no hand suffuses
But, dome-shadowed, withering among columns,
Wavy beneath fountains—small, far-off, shining
In the eyes of animals, these beings trapped
As I am trapped but not, themselves, the trap,
Aging, but without knowledge of their age,
Kept safe here, knowing not of death, for death—
Oh, bars of my own body, open, open!

The world goes by my cage and never sees me.
And there come not to me, as come to these,
The wild beasts, sparrows pecking the llamas' grain,
Pigeons settling on the bears' bread, buzzards
Tearing the meat the flies have clouded. . . .
                      Vulture,
When you come for the white rat that the foxes left,

Take off the red helmet of your head, the black
Wings that have shadowed me, and step to me as man:
The wild brother at whose feet the white wolves fawn,
To whose hand of power the great lioness
Stalks, purring. . . .
                    You know what I was,
You see what I am: change me, change me!

CINDERELLA

Her imaginary playmate was a grown-up
In sea-coal satin. The flame-blue glances,
The wings gauzy as the membrane that the ashes
Draw over an old ember—as the mother
In a jug of cider—were a comfort to her.
They sat by the fire and told each other stories.

"What men want. . . ." said the godmother softly—
How she went on it is hard for a man to say.
Their eyes, on their Father, were monumental marble.
Then they smiled like two old women, bussed each other,
Said, "Gossip, gossip"; and, lapped in each other's looks,
Mirror for mirror, drank a cup of tea.

Of cambric tea. But there is a reality
Under the good silk of the good sisters'
Good ball gowns. *She* knew. . . . Hard-breasted, naked-
    eyed,
She pushed her silk feet into glass, and rose within
A gown of imaginary gauze. The shy prince drank
A toast to her in champagne from her slipper

And breathed, "Bewitching!" Breathed, "I am bewitched!"
—She said to her godmother, "Men!"
And, later, looking down to see her flesh
Look back up from under lace, the ashy gauze
And pulsing marble of a bridal veil,
She wished it all a widow's coal-black weeds.

A sullen wife and a reluctant mother,
She sat all day in silence by the fire.

Better, later, to stare past her sons' sons,
Her daughters' daughters, and tell stories to the fire.
But best, dead, damned, to rock forever
Beside Hell's fireside—to see within the flames

The Heaven to whose gold-gauzed door there comes
A little dark old woman, the God's Mother,
And cries, "Come in, come in! My son's out now,
Out now, will be back soon, may be back never,
Who knows, eh? *We* know what they are—men, men!
But come, come in till then! Come in till then!"

THE END OF THE RAINBOW

Far from the clams and fogs and bogs
—The cranberry bogs—of Ipswich,
A sampler cast upon a savage shore,
There dwells in a turquoise, unfrequented store
A painter; a painter of land- and seascapes.

At nine o'clock, past Su-Su
—Asleep on the threshold, a spirited
Dwarf Pekinese, exceptionally loving—
The sun of Southern California streams
Unlovingly, but as though lovingly,
Upon the spare, paint-spotted and age-spotted hand's
Accustomed gesture.
                                Beyond the mahlstick a last wave
Breaks in Cobalt, Vert Emeraude, and Prussian Blue
Upon a Permanent White shore.

Her long hair, finer and redder once
Than the finest of red sable brushes, has been brushed
Till it is silver. The hairdresser, drunk with sunlight,
Has rinsed it a false blue. And blue
Are all the lights the seascapes cast upon it, blue
The lights the false sea casts upon it. Su-Su
—Su-Su is naturally black.

Five sheets of plate-glass, tinted green
And founded on the sand, now house the owner
Of the marsh-o'erlooking, silver-grey, unpainted salt-box
To which, sometimes, she writes a letter
—Home is where the dead are—

And goes with it, past CALIFORNIA,
And drops it in a mail-slot marked THE STATES.
The Frog-Prince, Marsh-King
Goggles at her from the bottom of the mail-slot.

There is brandy on his breath.
The cattails quivering above his brute
Imploring eyes, the tadpoles feathering
The rushes of his beard—black beard brought down
In silver to the grave—rustle again
In flaws or eddies of the wet wind: "Say.
Say. Say now. Say again."

                 She turns away
Into the irrigated land
With its blond hills like breasts of hay,
Its tall tan herds of eucalyptus grazing
Above its lawns of ice-plant, of geranium,
Its meadows of eternal asphodel.

The dark ghosts throng by
Shaking their locks at her—their fair, false locks—
Stretching out past her their bare hands, burnt hands.
And she—her face is masked, her hands are gloved
With a mask and gloves of bright brown leather:
The hands of a lady left out in the weather
Of resorts; the face of a fine girl left out in the years.

Voices float up: seals are barking
On the seal-rocks as, once, frogs were croaking
On rushy islands in the marsh of night.

Voices—the voices of others and her voice
Tuned flat like a country fiddle, like a Death

Rubbing his bow with resin at a square-dance—
Voices begin: . . . *A spider a frying-pan, and tonic pop,*
And—fancy!—put tomatoes in their chowder.
Go slow. Go slow. You owe it to yourself.
Watch out for the engine. You owe it to yourself.
Neither a borrower nor a lender be.
Better to be safe than sorry.
Better to be safe than sorry. Say to yourself,
Is it my money they're asking or me?
It must have been the money.
                                        The harsh
Voice goes on, blurred with darkness: *Cheat*
Or be cheaten. Let
And live let.

                    Great me. Great me. Great me.
Proverbs of the night
With the night's inconsequence, or consequence,
Sufficient unto the night. . . . *Every maid her own*
Merman—and she has left lonely forever,
Lonely forever, the kings of the marsh.
She says to Su-Su, "Come to your Content."
—*A name in the family for more*
Than seven generations. And Su-Su
—Su-Su is Su-Su IV.

Twelve o'clock: she locks
The door that she has painted, walks away
Straightforwardly, her Su-Su frisking
Before, on the leash that she has braided; eats
At a little table in a sunny courtyard
A date milkshake and an avocadoburger.

Thus evil communications
Corrupt good manners. . . .

                  Little Women, Little Men,
Upon what shores, pink-sanded, beside what cerulean
Seas have you trudged out, nodded over, napped away
Your medium-sized lives!

               Poor Water Babies
Who, summer evenings, sent to bed by sunlight,
Sat in your nightdress on a rag-rug island
Seeming some Pole, or Northwest Passage, or Hesperides
Of your bedchamber's humped, dark-shining Ocean:
The last sunbeam shone
Upon the marble set there at the center
Of that grey-glassed, black-eaved, white-dormered chamber
Until, not touched by any human hand,
Slowly,
Fast, faster, the red agate rolled
Into the humpbacked floor's scrubbed corner.
From your bed that night, you looked for it
And it was gone—gone, gone forever
Out into darkness, far from the warm flickering
Hemisphere the candle breathed
For you and your *Swiss Family Robinson*, marooned
With one down pillow on an uninhabited
Hair mattress. . . .

Su-Su is looking: it's the last of lunch.
She takes a piece of candy from her purse
—Dog-candy—and says, "Beg, sir!"
                    Su-Su begs.

9

They walk home in all amity, in firm
And literal association. She repeats: *With dogs
You know where you are;* and Su-Su's oil-brown,
                                                oil-blue stare
—The true Su-Su's true-blue stare—
Repeats: *With people you know where you are.*

Her thin feet, pointed neither out nor in
But straight before her, like an Indian's,
And set upon the path, a detour of the path
Of righteousness; her unaccommodating eyes'
Flat blue, matt blue
Or grey, depending on the point of view—
On whether one looks from here or from New England—
All these go unobserved, are unobservable:
She is old enough to be invisible.

Opening the belled door,
She turns once more to her new-framed, new-glassed
Landscape of a tree beside the sea.
It is light-struck.

If you look at a picture the wrong way
You see yourself instead.
                        —The wrong way?
A quarter of an hour and we tire
Of any landscape, said Goethe; eighty years
And he had not tired of Goethe. The landscape had,
And disposed of Goethe in the usual way.

She has looked into the mirror of the marsh
Flawed with the flight of dragonflies, the life of rushes,
And seen—what she had looked for—her own face

Staring up into her; but underneath,
In the depths of the dark water, witnessing
Unmoved, with a seal's angelic
More-than-human less-than-human eyes, a strange
Animal, some wizard ruling other realms,
The King of the Marsh.

                    She says: "He was a—*strange* man."

And the voice of a departed friend, a female
Friend, replies as crystal
Replies to a teaspoon, to a fingernail:
"A *strange* man. . . . But all men are, aren't they?
A man is like a merman." "A merman?"
"Mermen were seals, you know. They called them silkies."
"You mean the Forsaken Merman was a *seal?*"
"What did you think it was, a merman?
And mermaids were manatees." "The things you know!"
"The things you don't know!"

                  The Great Silkie,
His muzzle wide in love, holds out to her
His maimed flippers, and an uncontrollable
Shudder runs through her flesh, and she says, smiling:
"A goose was walking on my grave.
—And the Frog-Prince?" "Oh, I don't know.
If you ask me the Frog-Prince was a frog."

These days few men, few women, and no frogs
Enter "my little studio-shop," "my little paint-store,"
To buy paint; paintings; small black dogs;
Pieces of Pilgrim Rock; pomander-apples
In rosemary; agates; a marsh-violet pressed
In *Compensation*—red goatskin, India paper,

Inscribed in black ink, "For my loving daughter";
A miniature of Great-Great-Great-
Grandfather Wotkyns, pressed to death in Salem
For a wizard; a replica, life-sized, of a female friend
In crystal—wound, the works say, "Men!";
A framed poem signed *Beddoes:* she has dreams to sell.

She has spent her principal on dreams.
Some portion, though, is left—left to her in
                                        the Commonwealth
Of Massachusetts, in trust to the end of time.
But life, though, is not left in trust?
Life is not lived, in trust?
True, true—but how few live!
The gift for life, the gift of life
Are rarer, surely, than the gift of making
In a life-class, a study from the life
Of some girl naked for an hour, by the hour;
Of making, from an egg, a jug,
An eggplant, at cross-purposes on drapery,
A still-life; of rendering, with a stump,
Art-gum, and four hardnesses of charcoal, life
Whispering to the naked girl, the naked egg, the naked
Painter: "What am I offered for this frog?"

A kiss? The Frog-Prince, kissed,
Is a prince indeed; a king, a husband, and a father;
According to his State, a citizen; according to
                                        his God, a soul;
According to his—*fiancée,* a risk
Uncalculated, incalculable; a load
Whose like she will not look upon again; a responsibility
She is no longer saddled with, praise Heaven!

[Applause.] And, smiling as she used to smile,
She murmurs as she used to murmur: "Men!"

She looks into the mirror and says: "Mirror,
Who is the fairest of us all?"

According to the mirror, it's the mirror.

Great me. Great me. Great me. The voices tune themselves
And keep on tuning: there is no piece, just tuning.
. . . But there are compensations; there is *Compensation.*
She reads it (it, or else the Scriptures
With a *Key* by Mrs. Eddy) when she wakes
In the night as she so often does: the earth
Lies light upon the old, and they are wakeful.

She reads patiently: the bed-lamp lights
Above her sunlit, moonlit, starlit bed
The little slogan under which she sleeps
Or is wakeful: HE WHO HAS HIMSELF FOR FRIEND
IS BEST BEFRIENDED—this in gothic.
One sees, through the bars of the first *H*, a landscape
Manned with men, womaned with women,
                                        dogged with a dog,
And influenced—Content says—by the influence
Of *The Very Rich Hours of the Duke of Burgundy.*
The hours of the earth
—The very rich hours, the very poor hours,
                              the very long hours—
Go by, and she is wakeful.

She wakes, sometimes, when she has met a friend
In the water; he is just standing in the water, bathing.
He has shaved now, and smells of peppermint.

He holds out to her
With hands like hip-boots, like her father's waders,
A corsage of watercress: the white bridal-veil-lace flowers
Are shining with water-drops. In their clear depths
She sees, like so many cupids, water babies:
Little women, little men.
He pulls his feet with a slow sucking sound
From the floor where he is stuck, like a horse in concrete,
And, reaching to her, whispers patiently
—Whispers, or the wind whispers, water whispers: "Say.
Say. Say now. Say again."

            A slow
Delicious shudder runs along her spine:
She takes off her straw sailor.
Red again, and long enough to sit on,
Her hair floats out to him—and, slowly,
                           she holds out to him
In their white, new-washed gloves, her dry
Brown leather hands, and whispers: "Father,
If you come any closer I'll call Father."

He melts, in dark drops, to a little dark
Pool drying on the floor, to Su-Su. It is Su-Su!
She holds out to the little dark
Grave drying in the grass, her little dry
Bouquet of ice-plant, of geranium,
And reads: *In Loving Memory of Su-Su*
I, II, III, IV.
She says: "That four is a mistake.
One two three is right, but leave out four."

The Prince is dead. . . . The willows waver
Above the cresses of his tomb. .

—His tomb?
The Frog-Prince is married to a frog, has little frogs,
Says sometimes, after dinner, in his den:
"There was a mortal once. . . ." And his Content
Goes through the suburbs with a begging-bowl
Of teak, a Wedgewood cowbell, ringing, ringing,
Calling: *Untouched! Untouched!*
                    The doors shut themselves
Not helped by any human hand, mail-boxes
Pull down their flags, the finest feelers
Of the television sets withdraw.
                  Beside her, Death
Or else Life—spare, white, permanent—
Works out their *pas de deux:* here's Death
Arranging a still-life for his own Content;
Death walking Su-Su; Death presenting
To the trustees of the estate, a varied
Portfolio; Death digging
For gold at the end of the rainbow—strikes water,
Which is thinner than blood; strikes oil,
That water will not mix with—no, nor blood;
Pauses, mops his skull, says: *The wrong end.*

At home in Massachusetts gold, red gold
Gushes above the Frog-Prince, Princess, all the Princelets
Digging with sand-pails, tiny shovels, spoons, a porringer
Planned, ages since, by Paul Revere. They call:
                  "Come play! Come play!"
Death breaks the ice
On her Hopi jar and washes out the brushes;
Says, as he hands her them: *Life's work. It's work.*
Out here at the wrong end of the rainbow
Say to yourself: What's a rainbow anyway?

She looks into the mirror, through the rainbow
—The little home-made rainbow, there in tears—
And hears the voices the years shatter into
As the sunlight shatters into colors: *Me. Me. Me,*
The voices tune themselves.
She says: "Look at my life. Should I go on with it?
It seems to you I have . . . a real gift?
I shouldn't like to keep on if I only. . . .
It seems to you my life is a success?"

Death answers, *Yes. Well, yes.*

She looks around her:
Many waves are breaking on many shores,
The wind turns over, absently,
The leaves of a hundred thousand trees.
How many colors, squeezed from how many tubes
In patient iteration, have made up the world
She draws closer, like a patchwork quilt,
To warm her, all the warm, long, summer day!
The local colors fade:
She hangs here on the verge of seeing
In black and white,
And turns with an accustomed gesture
To the easel, saying:
"Without my paintings I would be—
                    why, whatever *would* I be?"

Safe from all the nightmares
One comes upon awake in the world, she sleeps.
She sleeps in sunlight, surrounded by many dreams
Or dreams of dreams, all good—how can a dream be bad
If it keeps one asleep?

The unpeopled landscapes
Run down to the seal-less, the merman-less seas,
And she rolls softly, like an agate, down to Su-Su
Asleep upon the doorsill of the seas.
The first Su-Su, the second Su-Su, the third Su-Su
Are dead?
Long live Su-Su IV!

The little black dog sleeping in the doorway
Of the little turquoise store, can dream
His own old dream: that he is sleeping
In the doorway of the little turquoise store.

IN THOSE DAYS

In those days—they were long ago—
The snow was cold, the night was black.
I licked from my cracked lips
A snowflake, as I looked back

Through branches, the last uneasy snow.
Your shadow, there in the light, was still.
In a little the light went out.
I went on, stumbling—till at last the hill

Hid the house. And, yawning,
In bed in my room, alone,
I would look out: over the quilted
Rooftops, the clear stars shone.

How poor and miserable we were,
How seldom together!
And yet after so long one thinks:
In those days everything was better.

THE ELEMENTARY SCENE

Looking back in my mind I can see
The white sun like a tin plate
Over the wooden turning of the weeds;
The street jerking—a wet swing—
To end by the wall the children sang.

The thin grass by the girls' door,
Trodden on, straggling, yellow and rotten,
And the gaunt field with its one tied cow—
The dead land waking sadly to my life—
Stir, and curl deeper in the eyes of time.

The rotting pumpkin under the stairs
Bundled with switches and the cold ashes
Still holds for me, in its unwavering eyes,
The stinking shapes of cranes and witches,
Their path slanting down the pumpkin's sky.

Its stars beckon through the frost like cottages
(Homes of the Bear, the Hunter—of that absent star,
The dark where the flushed child struggles into sleep)
Till, leaning a lifetime to the comforter,
I float above the small limbs like their dream:

I, I, the future that mends everything.

WINDOWS

Quarried from snow, the dark walks lead to doors
That are dark and closed. The white- and high-roofed
   houses
Float in the moonlight of the shining sky
As if they slept, the bedclothes pulled around them.
But in some the lights still burn. The lights of others' houses.

Those who live there move seldom, and are silent.
Their movements are the movements of a woman darning,
A man nodding into the pages of the paper,
And are portions of a rite—have kept a meaning—
That I, that they know nothing of. What I have never heard
He will read me; what I have never seen
She will show me.
                        As dead actors, on a rainy afternoon,
Move in a darkened living-room, for children
Watching the world that was before they were,
The windowed ones within their windowy world
Move past me without doubt and for no reason.

These actors, surely, have known nothing of today,
That time of troubles and of me. Of troubles.
Morose and speechless, voluble with elation,
Changing, unsleeping, an unchanging speech,
These have not lived; look up, indifferent,
At me at my window, from the snowy walk
They move along in peace. . . . If only I were they!
Could act out, in longing, the impossibility
That haunts me like happiness!

Of so many windows, one is always open.

Some morning they will come downstairs and find me.
They will start to speak, and then smile speechlessly,
Shifting the plates, and set another place
At a table shining by a silent fire.
When I have eaten they will say, "You have not slept."

And from the sofa, mounded in my quilt,
My face on *their* pillow, that is always cool,
I will look up speechlessly into a—

It blurs, and there is drawn across my face
As my eyes close, a hand's slow fire-warmed flesh.

It moves so slowly that it does not move.

AGING

I wake, but before I know it it is done,
The day, I sleep. And of days like these the years,
A life is made. I nod, consenting to my life.
. . . But who can live in these quick-passing hours?
I need to find again, to make a life,
A child's Sunday afternoon, the Pleasure Drive
Where everything went by but time; the Study Hour
Spent at a desk, with folded hands, in waiting.

In those I could make. Did I not make in them
Myself? The Grown One whose time shortens,
Breath quickens, heart beats faster, till at last
It catches, skips. . . . Yet those hours that seemed, were
    endless
Were still not long enough to have remade
My childish heart: the heart that must have, always,
To make anything of anything, not time,
Not time but—
                but, alas! eternity.

NESTUS GURLEY

Sometimes waking, sometimes sleeping,
Late in the afternoon, or early
In the morning, I hear on the lawn,
On the walk, on the lawn, the soft quick step,
The sound half song, half breath: a note or two
That with a note or two would be a tune.
It is Nestus Gurley.

It is an old
Catch or snatch or tune
In the Dorian mode: the mode of the horses
That stand all night in the fields asleep
Or awake, the mode of the cold
Hunter, Orion, wheeling upside-down,
All space and stars, in cater-cornered Heaven.
When, somewhere under the east,
The great march begins, with birds and silence;
When, in the day's first triumph, dawn
Rides over the houses, Nestus Gurley
Delivers to me my lot.

As the sun sets, I hear my daughter say:
"He has four routes and makes a hundred dollars."
Sometimes he comes with dogs, sometimes with children,
Sometimes with dogs and children.
He collects, today.
I hear my daughter say:
"Today Nestus has got on his derby."
And he says, after a little: "It's two-eighty."
"How could it be two-eighty?"

"Because this month there're five Sundays: it's two-
    eighty."

He collects, delivers. Before the first, least star
Is lost in the paling east; at evening
While the soft, side-lit, gold-leafed day
Lingers to see the stars, the boy Nestus
Delivers to me the Morning Star, the Evening Star
—Ah no, only the Morning *News*, the Evening *Record*
Of what I have done and what I have not done
Set down and held against me in the Book
Of Death, on paper yellowing
Already, with one morning's sun, one evening's sun.

Sometimes I only dream him. He brings then
News of a different morning, a judgment not of men.
The bombers have turned back over the Pole,
Having met a star. . . . I look at that new year
And, waking, think of our Moravian Star
Not lit yet, and the pure beeswax candle
With its red flame-proofed paper pompom
Not lit yet, and the sweetened
Bun we brought home from the love-feast, still not eaten,
And the song the children sang: *O Morning Star*—

And at this hour, to the dew-hushed drums
Of the morning, Nestus Gurley
Marches to me over the lawn; and the cat Elfie,
Furred like a musk-ox, coon-tailed, gold-leaf-eyed,
Looks at the paper boy without alarm
But yawns, and stretches, and walks placidly
Across the lawn to his ladder, climbs it, and begins to
    purr.

24

I let him in,
Go out and pick up from the grass the paper hat
Nestus has folded: this tricorne fit for a Napoleon
Of our days and institutions, weaving
Baskets, being bathed, receiving
Electric shocks, Rauwolfia. . . . I put it on
—Ah no, only unfold it.
There is dawn inside; and I say to no one
About—
        it is a note or two
That with a note or two would—
                say to no one
About nothing: "He delivers dawn."

When I lie coldly
—Lie, that is, neither with coldness nor with warmth—
In the darkness that is not lit by anything,
In the grave that is not lit by anything
Except our hope: the hope
That is not proofed against anything, but pure
And shining as the first, least star
That is lost in the east on the morning of Judgment—
May I say, recognizing the step
Or tune or breath. . . .
            recognizing the breath,
May I say, "It is Nestus Gurley."

THE GREAT NIGHT

(*Rainer Maria Rilke*)

Often I looked at you—stood at the window I had started
The day before, stood and looked at you. The new city
    still
Seemed something forbidden; the landscape, not yet won
    over,
Darkened as though I was not. The closest things
Didn't bother to make me understand. The street
Crowded itself up to the lamp post; I saw that it was
    strange.
Out there a room was clear in lamplight—
Already I was part; they sensed it, closed the shutters.
I stood there. And then a child cried. And I knew
The mothers in the houses, what they were—knew, sud-
    denly,
The spring of all our tears, the spring that is never dry.
Or a voice sang, and went a little beyond
Whatever I had expected; or an old man coughed,
Full of reproach, as though his flesh were in the right
Against the gentler world. Then a clock struck the hour—
But I counted too late, and it got by me.
As a boy, a stranger, when at last they let him,
Can't catch the ball, and doesn't know any of the games
The others are playing together so easily,
So that he stands and looks off—where?—I stand, and
    suddenly
See that *you* have made friends with me, played with me,
    grown-up
Night, and I look at you. While the towers
Were angered, while with averted fates

A city encompassed me, and the unguessable hills
Were encamped against me, and in closing circles
Strangeness hungered round the chance-set flares
Of my senses: then was it, O highest,
That you felt it no shame to know me, that your breath
Went over me, that there passed into me
Your grave and from far apportioning smile.

THE GROWN-UP

(*Rainer Maria Rilke*)

All this stood on her and was the world,
And stood on her with all things, Pain and Grace,
As trees stand, growing and erect, all image
And imageless as the ark of the Lord God,
And solemn, as if set upon a State.

And she bore it; bore, somehow, the weight
Of the flying, fleeting, far-away,
The monstrous and the still-unmastered,
Unmoved, serene, as the water-bearer
Stands under a full jar. Till in the midst of play,
Transfiguring, preparing for the Other,
The first white veil fell smoothly, softly,

Over her opened face, almost opaque,
Never to raise itself again, and giving somehow
To all her questions one vague answer:
In thee, thou once a child, in thee.

WASHING THE CORPSE

(*Rainer Maria Rilke*)

They had got used to him. But when they brought
The kitchen lamp in, and it was burning
Uneasily in the dark air, the stranger
Was altogether strange. They washed his neck,

And since they had no knowledge of his fate
They lied till they had put together one,
Always washing. One of them had to cough,
And while she was coughing she left the heavy

Sponge of vinegar on his face. The other
Stopped a minute too, and the drops knocked
From the hard brush, while his dreadful
Cramped hand wanted to demonstrate
To the whole household that he no longer thirsted.

And he did demonstrate it. Coughing shortly,
As if embarrassed, they went back to work
More hurriedly now, so that across the dumb
Pattern of the wallpaper their contorted shadows

Writhed and wallowed as though in a net
Until the washing reached its end.
The night, in the uncurtained window-frame,
Was relentless. And one without a name
Lay clean and naked there, and gave commandments.

EVENING

(Rainer Maria Rilke)

The evening folds about itself the dark
Garments the old trees hold out to it.
You watch: and the lands are borne from you,
One soaring heavenward, one falling;

And leave you here, not wholly either's,
Not quite so darkened as the silent houses,
Not quite so surely summoning the eternal
As that which each night becomes star, and rises;

And leave you (inscrutably to unravel)
Your life: the fearful and ripening and enormous
Being that—bounded by everything, or boundless—
For a moment becomes stone, for a moment stars.

CHILDHOOD

(adapted from Rainer Maria Rilke)

The time of school drags by with waiting
And dread, with nothing but dreary things.
O loneliness, O leaden waiting-out of time. . . .
And then out. The streets are gleaming and ringing,
All the fountains flash up from the squares.
In the parks the world is enormous.
And to walk through it all in one's little suit
Not at all as the others go, have ever gone:
O miraculous time, O waiting-out of time,
O loneliness.

And to gaze far out into it all:
Men and women, men, men—black and tall
And going slowly, as if in their sleep,
Beside the sudden white and blue and red
Children; a house here, now and then a dog,
And one's fear changing silently to trust:
O senseless grief, O dream, O dread,
O bottomless abyss.

And then to play with top or hoop or ball
Beneath the paling branches of the park
Or sometimes, blind and wild in the reeling
Rush of tag, to brush against the grown-ups,
But to go home with them when it is dark
With little stiff steps, quiet, held fast to:
O knowledge ever harder to hold fast to,
O dread, O burden.

And to kneel beside the great gray pond
Hour on hour with one's little sail-boat,
Forgetting it because so many more,
Lovely and lovelier, glide through darkening rings,
And to have to think about the little pale
Face that shone up from the water, sinking:
O childhood, O images gliding from us
Somewhere. But where? But where?

LAMENT

(*Rainer Maria Rilke*)

All is far
And long gone by.
I believe the star
That shines up there
Has been dead for a thousand years.
I believe, in the car
I heard go by,
Something terrible was said.
In the house a clock
Is striking. . . .
In what house?
I would like to walk
Out of my heart, under the great sky.
I would like to pray.
And surely, of all the stars,
One still must be.
I believe I know
Which one endures;
Which one, at the end of its beam in the sky,
Stands like a white city.

THE CHILD

(*Rainer Maria Rilke*)

Without meaning to, they watch him play
A long time; once or twice his profile
Turns and becomes a live, full face—
Clear and entire as a completed

Hour that is raised to strike its end.
But the others do not count the strokes.
Exhausted with misery, enduring their lives,
They do not even see that he endures:

Endures everything, now and always,
As—near them, as though in a waiting-room,
Wearily, dressed in his little dress—
He sits and waits till his time comes.

DEATH

(*Rainer Maria Rilke*)

There stands death, a bluish liquid
In a cup without a saucer.
An odd place for a cup:
Stands on the back of a hand. And one can see
Quite plainly, there on the glassy slope,
The place where the handle broke off. Dusty. And HOPE
On the side in used-up letters.

The drinker that drank the drink
Read it out, long, long ago, at breakfast.

This being of theirs!
To get rid of them you have to poison them?

Except for that, they'd stay? They munch away
At their own frustration so insatiably?
One has to pull the present from their mouths,
The hard present, like a dental plate.

Then they mumble. Mumble, mumble. . . .

. . . .
Star
Seen from a bridge once: O falling star,
Not to forget you. Stand!

REQUIEM
FOR THE DEATH OF A BOY

(*Rainer Maria Rilke*)

Why did I print upon myself the names
Of Elephant and Dog and Cow
So far off now, already so long ago,
And Zebra, too. . . . what for, what for?
What holds me now
Climbs like a water line
Up past all that. What help was it to know
I was, if I could never press
Through what's soft, what's hard, and come at last
Behind them, to the face that understands?

And these beginning hands—

Sometimes you'd say: "He promises. . . ."
Yes, I promised. But what I promised you,
That was never what I felt afraid of.
Sometimes I'd sit against the house for hours
And look up at a bird.
If only I could have turned into the looking!
It lifted me, it flew me, how my eyes
Were open up there then! But I didn't love anybody.
Loving was misery—
Don't you see, I wasn't we,
And I was so much bigger
Than a man, I was my own danger,
And, inside it, I was the seed.

A little seed. The street can have it.
The wind can have it. I give it away.

Because that we all sat there so together—
I never did believe that. No, honestly.
You talked, you laughed, but none of you were ever
Inside the talking or the laughing. No.
The sugar bowl, a glass of milk
Would never waver the way you would waver.
The apple lay there. Sometimes it felt so good
To hold tight to it, a hard ripe apple.
The big table, the coffee-cups that never moved—
They were good, how peaceful they made the year!
And my toy did me good too, sometimes.
It was as reliable, almost, as the others,
Only not so peaceful. It stood halfway
Between me and my hat, in watchfulness forever.
There was a wooden horse, there was a rooster,
There was the doll with only one leg.
I did so much for them.
I made the sky small when they saw it
Because almost from the start I understood
How alone a wooden horse is. You can make one,
A wooden horse, one any size.
It gets painted, and later on you pull it,
And it's the real street it pounds down, then.
When you call it a horse, why isn't it a lie?
Because you feel that you're a horse, a little,
And grow all maney, shiny, grow four legs—
So as to grow, some day, into a man?
But wasn't I wood a little, too,
For its sake, and grew hard and quiet
And looked out at it from an emptier face?

I almost think we traded places.
Whenever I would see the brook I'd race it,

And the brook raced, too, and I would run away.
Whenever I saw something that could ring, I rang,
And whenever something sang I played for it.

I made myself at home with everything.
Only everything was satisfied without me
And got sadder, hung about with me.

Now, all at once, we're separated.
Do the lessons and the questions start again?
Or, now, ought I to say
What it was like with you?—That worries me.
The house? I never got it right, exactly.
The rooms? Oh, there were so many things, so many.
. . . Mother, *who* was the dog really?
That in the forest we would come on berries—
Even that seems, now, extraordinary.

Surely there're some other children
Who've died, to come play with me. They're always
    dying;
Lie there in bed, like me, and never do get well.

Well. . . . How funny that sounds, here.
Does it mean something, still?
Here where I am
No one is ill, I think.
Since my sore throat, so long ago already—

Here everyone is like a just-poured drink.

But the ones who drink us I still haven't seen.

THE WINTER'S TALE

(*Henrikas Radauskas*)

Guess what smells so. . . . You didn't guess.
Lilies? Lindens? No. Winds? No.
But princes and barbers smell so,
The evening smells so, in a dream.

Look: a line goes through the glass
Bending quietly; and the hushed
Light, in the tender mist,
Is gurgling like a brook of milk.

Look: it's snowing, it's snowing, it's snowing.
Look: the white orchard is falling asleep.
The earth has sunk into the past.
Guess who's coming. . . . You didn't guess.
Princes and barbers are coming,
White kings and bakers,
And the trees murmur, covered with snow.

THE ARCHANGELS' SONG

(*from Goethe's* FAUST)

RAPHAEL:

> The sun sings out, as of old,
> Against the spheres' unchanging sound;
> Yet once more, with thunderous footsteps,
> He works out his predestined round.
> Though no angel fathoms him, his face
> Gives strength to them upon their way;
> The inconceivably exalted works
> Are glorious as on the first day.

GABRIEL:

> Swift, past all understanding swift
> Is the splendor of earth's whirling flight:
> The brilliance of Paradise is changed
> For the awful darkness of the night.
> The ocean foams up, overwhelming,
> The great rocks tremble with the force,
> And rocks and ocean are swept onward
> In the spheres' swift, eternal course.

MICHAEL:

> In rivalry the tempests roar
> From sea to land, from land to sea,
> And, raging, forge out for the earth
> Fetters of wildest energy.
> Before the path of the thunderbolt
> The lightnings of desolation blaze.
> And yet thine angels, Lord, adore
> The tranquil footsteps of thy days.

ALL THREE:

Since none can fathom thee, thy face
Gives strength to us upon our way,
And thine exalted works, O God,
Are glorious as on the first day.

FOREST MURMURS

(*Eduard Mörike*)

Stretched out under the oak, in the wood's new leaves,
I lay with my book. To me it is still the sweetest;

All the fairy tales are in it, the Goose Girl and the Juniper
    Tree
And the Fisherman's Wife—truly, one never gets tired of
    them.

The curly light flung down to me its green May-shine,
Flung on the shadowy book its mischievous illustrations.

I heard, far away, the strokes of the axe; heard the cuckoo
And the rippling of the brook, a step or two beyond.

I myself felt like a fairy tale; with new-washed senses
I saw, O so clear! the forest, the cuckoo called, O so
    strange!

All at once the leaves rustle—isn't it Snow-White coming
Or some enchanted stag? Oh no, it's nothing miraculous:

See, my neighbor's child from the village, my good little
    sweetheart!
She'd nothing to do, and ran to the forest to her father.

Demurely she seats herself at my side, confidentially
We gossip of this and that; and I tell her the story

(Leaving out nothing) of the sorrows of that incom-
    parable
Maiden her mother three times threatened with death.

Because she was so beautiful, the Queen, the vain one,
    hated her
Fiercely, so that she fled, made her home with dwarfs.

But soon the Queen found her; knocked at the door as a
    peddler,
Craftily offering the girl her wonderful things to buy;

And forgetting the words of the dwarfs, the innocent
    child
Let her in—and the dear thing bought, alas! the poisoned
    comb.

What a wailing there is that night, when the little ones
    come home!
What work it takes, what skill, before the sleeper awakes!

But now a second time, a third time, in disguise,
The destroyer comes. How easily she persuades the
    maiden;

Laces in the tender body, strangling it, till she has choked
The breath in the breast; brings, last, the deadly fruit.

Now nothing is any help; how the dwarfs weep!
The poor darling is locked in a crystal coffin, they set it

There on the mountain side in sight of all the stars—
And inside it, unfading forever, the sweet shape sleeps.

So far had I come: all at once, from the thicket behind
    me,
The song of the nightingale arose in radiant splendor,

Rained through the boughs like honey, sprinkling its fiery
Barbed sounds down over me; I shuddered in terror, in
     delight—

So one of the goddesses, flying above him unseen,
Betrays herself to a poet with her ambrosial fragrance.

But soon, alas! the singer was silent. I listened a long time
But in vain; and so I brought my story to its end.—

Just then the child pointed and cried: "She's here already,
It's Margaret! See, she's brought Father the milk, in her
     basket."

Through the branches I could make out her older sister;
Leaving the meadow, she had turned up into the wood.

Bronzed and stalwart, the maid; noon blazed on her
     cheeks.
We'd have frightened her if we could, but she greeted us
     first:

"Come along, if you like! Today you don't need any meat
Or soup, it's so warm. My meal is rich and cool."

And I didn't struggle. We followed the sound of the
     wood-axe.
How willingly I should have led, instead of the child, her
     sister!

Friend, you honor the Muse who, ages ago, to thousands
Told her stories, but now for a long time has been silent.

Who by the winter fireside, the loom and the work-bench,
Proffered to the folk's creating wit her delectable food.

Her kingdom is the impossible: impudent, frivolous, she
  ladles together
All that's unlikeliest, gleefully gives her prizes to half-wits.

Allowed three wishes, her hero will pick the silliest.
To honor her, now, let me make to you this confession—

How at the side of the girl, the sweet-spoken, the never-
  silent,
Catching me unawares, the passionate wish overwhelmed
  me:

If I were a hunter, a shepherd, if I were born a peasant,
If I handled an axe, a shovel—you, Margaret, would be
  my wife!

Never then would I complain of the heat of the day;
The plainest food, if you served it, would seem a feast.

Each morning, in its magnificence, the sun would meet
  me—
Each evening, in magnificence, blaze over the ripening
  fields.

Fresh from the woman's kiss, my blood would grow sweet
  as balsam;
Boisterous with children, my house would blossom on
  high.

But on winter nights, when the drifts pile high—by the
  fireside,
O Muse, maker of the stories of men! I would invoke
  thee.

JAMESTOWN

Let me look at what I was, before I die.
Strange, that one's photograph in kindergarten
Is a captain in a ruff and a Venusian
—Is nothing here American?
John Smith is squashed
Beneath the breasts of Pocahontas: some true Christian,
Engraving all, has made the captain Man,
The maiden the most voluptuous of newts.
Met in a wood and lain with, this red demon,
The mother of us all, lies lovingly
Upon the breastplate of our father: the First Family
Of Jamestown trembles beneath the stone
Axe—then Powhatan, smiling, gives the pair his blessing
And nymphs and satyrs foot it at their wedding.
The continents, like country children, peep in awe
As Power, golden as a Veronese,
Showers her riches on the lovers: Nature,
Nature at last is married to a man.

The two lived happily
Forever after. . . . And I only am escaped alone
To tell the story. But how shall I tell the story?
The settlers died? All settlers die. The colony
Was a Lost Colony? All colonies are lost.
John Smith and Pocahontas, carving on a tree
We Have Gone Back For More People, crossed the sea
And were put to death, for treason, in the Tower
Of London? Ah, but they needed no one!
Powhatan,
Smiling at that red witch, red·wraith, his daughter,

Said to the father of us all, John Smith:
"American,
To thyself be enough! . . ." He was enough—
Enough, or too much. The True Historie
Of the Colony of Jamestown is a wish.

Long ago, hundreds of years ago, a man
Met a woman in a wood, a witch.
The witch said, "Wish!"
The man said, "Make me what I am."
The witch said, "Wish again!"
The man said, "Make me what I am."
The witch said, "For the last time, wish!"
The man said, "Make me what I am."
The witch said: "Mortal, because you have believed
In your mortality, there is no wood, no wish,
No world, there is only you. But what are you?
The world has become you. But what are you?
Ask;
Ask, while the time to ask remains to you."

The witch said, smiling: "This is Jamestown.
From Jamestown, Virginia, to Washington, D.C.,
Is, as the rocket flies, eleven minutes."

THE LONELY MAN

A cat sits on the pavement by the house.
It lets itself be touched, then slides away.
A girl goes by in a hood; the winter noon's
Long shadows lengthen. The cat is gray,
It sits there. It sits there all day, every day.

A collie bounds into my arms: he is a dog
And, therefore, finds nothing human alien.
He lives at the preacher's with a pair of cats.
The soft half-Persian sidles to me;
Indoors, the old white one watches blindly.

How cold it is! Some snow slides from a roof
When a squirrel jumps off it to a squirrel-proof
Feeding-station; and, a lot and two yards down,
A fat spaniel snuffles out to me
And sobers me with his untrusting frown.

He worries about his yard: past it, it's my affair
If I halt Earth in her track—his duty's done.
And the cat and the collie worry about the old one:
They come, when she's out too, so uncertainly. . . .
It's my block; I know them, just as they know me.

As for the others, those who wake up every day
And feed these, keep the houses, ride away
To work—I don't know them, they don't know me.
Are we friends or enemies? Why, who can say?
We nod to each other sometimes, in humanity,

Or search one another's faces with a yearning
Remnant of faith that's almost animal. . . .
The gray cat that just sits there: surely it is learning
To be a man; will find, soon, *some especial*
Opening in a good firm for a former cat.

THE TRAVELER

As she rides to the station
There is always something she has left behind.
Here is her hatbox; where is her hat?
Or she is blind—but the others are blind,
Not one thinks: Where are her eyes?
This plush smells—how does she smell it?
Her head hangs on a hanger in the closet
And calls as an engine calls, the engine
Cries as a head cries: *Shall I spare this city?*
The rails answer: *Raze it, raze it.*
She thinks as a child thinks:
When the sun sets, it is to count my loss.

Here in the station, in the other station,
On the track, appearing each instant,
That is made to her destination,
Her purse is heavier than she can know,
Her streaked breasts shake with a double heart.
When she steps at last to the stone of the station
Her arm drags, her step is slow.
She carries her head in her hand like a hatbox
Of money, of paper money:
A headful of money not even she will take.

When the moon rises, it is to count her money.
She sits on the bed of a bedroom counting her money:
Her look glazes, her breath is slow.
The wind moves to her
Softly, through parting curtains,

And a bill on the floor, a bill on the comfort,
As though they were living, stir.
When the wind says, *Shall I spare this city?*
She gives no answer.

A GHOST, A REAL GHOST

I think of that old woman in the song
Who could not know herself without the skirt
They cut off while she slept beside a stile.
Her dog jumped at the unaccustomed legs
And barked till she turned slowly from her gate
And went—I never asked them where she went.

The child is hopeful and unhappy in a world
Whose future is his recourse: she kept walking
Until the skirt grew, cleared her head and dog—
Surely I thought so when I laughed. If skirts don't grow,
If things can happen so, and you not know
What you could do, why, what is there you could do?

I know now she went nowhere; went to wait
In the bare night of the fields, to whisper:
"I'll sit and wish that it was never so."
I see her sitting on the ground and wishing,
The wind jumps like a dog against her legs,
And she keeps thinking: "This is all a dream.

"Who would cut off a poor old woman's skirt?
So good too. No, it's not so:
No one could feel so, really." And yet one might.
A ghost must; and she was, perhaps, a ghost.
The first night I looked into the mirror
And saw the room empty, I could not believe

That it was possible to keep existing
In such pain: I have existed.

Was the old woman dead? What does it matter?
—Am I dead? A ghost, a real ghost
Has no need to die: what is he except
A being without access to the universe
That he has not yet managed to forget?

THE METEORITE

Star, that looked so long among the stones
And picked from them, half iron and half dirt,
One; and bent and put it to her lips
And breathed upon it till at last it burned
Uncertainly, among the stars its sisters—
Breathe on me still, star, sister.

CHARLES DODGSON'S SONG

The band played *Idomeneo:*
  A child's felicity
Held Stendhal, sitting with the Empress
  Eugenie on his fat knee.

Clerk Maxwell's demon was possessed;
  He lay for half his days
And never moved a single molecule.
  Mill, haunted by the silent face

Of Bentham—it was made of wax—
  Read Wordsworth, and at last could weep.
I sought for love, and found it in girls' gloves:
  There's none outside, you know. "That bird's dead,
    Father,"

Said Darwin's son. Dejectedly
  The Father broke his spear, looked deep
Into the Cause of things: but it was only
  A hippopotamus asleep.

DEUTSCH DURCH FREUD

I believe my favorite country's German.

I wander in a calm folk-colored daze; the infant
Looks down upon me from his mother's arms
And says—oh, God knows what he says!
It's baby-talk? he's sick? or is it German?
That *Nachtigallenchor:* does it sing German?
Yoh, yoh: here mice, rats, tables, chairs,
Grossmütter, Kinder, der Herrgott im Himmel,
All, all but I—
    all, all but I—
       speak German.

Have you too sometimes, by the fire, at evening,
Wished that you were—whatever you once were?
It is ignorance alone that is enchanting.
*Dearer to me than all the treasures of the earth
Is something living,* said old Rumpelstiltskin
And hopped home. Charcoal-burners heard him singing
And spoiled it all. . . . And all because—
If only he hadn't known his name!

In German I don't know my name.
        I am the log
The fairies left one morning in my place.
—In German I believe in them, in everything:
The world is everything that is the case.
How clever people are! I look on open-mouthed
As Kant reels down the road *im Morgenrot*
Humming *Mir ist so bang, so bang, mein Schatz—*
All the nixies set their watches by him

56

Two hours too fast. . . .
                          I think, *My calendar's*
Two centuries too fast, and give a sigh
Of trust. I reach out for the world and ask
The price; it answers, *One touch of your finger*.

In all *my* Germany there's no *Gesellschaft*
But one between *eine Katze* and *ein Maus*.
What's business? what's a teaspoon? what's a sidewalk?
Schweig stille, meine Seele! Such things are not for thee.
It is by Trust, and Love, and reading Rilke
Without *ein Wörterbuch*, that man learns German.
The Word rains in upon his blessed head
As glistening as from the hand of God
And means—what does it mean? Ah well, it's German.
Glaube, mein Herz! A Feeling in the Dark
Brings worlds, brings words that hard-eyed Industry
And all the schools' dark Learning never knew.

And yet it's hard sometimes, I won't deny it.
Take for example my own favorite daemon,
Dear good great Goethe: *ach*, what German!
Very idiomatic, very noble; very like a sibyl.
My favorite style is Leupold von Lerchenau's.
I've memorized his *da und da und da und da*
And whisper it when Life is dark and Death is dark.
There was someone who knew how to speak
To us poor *Kinder* here *im Fremde*.
And Heine! At the ninety-sixth *mir träumte*
I sigh as a poet, but dimple as *ein Schuler*.
And yet—if it's easy is it German?
And yet, that *wunderschöne Lindenbaum*
Im Mondenscheine! What if it is in Schilda?

It's moonlight, isn't it? *Mund, Mond, Herz,* and *Schmerz*
Sing round my head, in *Zeit* and *Ewigkeit,*
And my heart lightens at each *Sorge,* each *Angst:*
I know them well. And *Schicksal! Ach,* you Norns,
As I read I hear your—what's the word for scissors?
And *Katzen* have *Tatzen*—why can't I call someone
    Kind?
What a speech for Poetry (especially Folk-)!

And yet when, in my dreams, *eine schwartzbraune Hexe*
(Who mows on the Neckar, reaps upon the Rhine)
Riffles my yellow ringlets through her fingers,
She only asks me questions: *What is soap?*
I don't know. *A suitcase?* I don't know. *A visit?*
I laugh with joy, and try to say like Lehmann:
"*Quin-quin, es ist ein Besuch!*"
                                        Ah, German!
Till the day I die I'll be in love with German
—If only I don't learn German. . . . I can hear my
    broken
Voice murmuring to *der Arzt: "Ich—sterber?"*
He answers sympathetically: "*Nein—sterbe.*"

If God gave me the choice—but I stole this from
    Lessing—
Of German and learning German, I'd say: Keep your
    German!

The thought of *knowing* German terrifies me.
—But surely, this way, no one could learn German?
And yet. . . .
                    It's difficult; is it impossible?
I'm hopeful that it is, but I can't say
For certain: I don't know enough German.

THE GIRL DREAMS THAT
SHE IS GISELLE

Beards of the grain, gray-green: the lances
Shiver. I stare up into the dew.
From her white court—enchantress—
The black queen, shimmering with dew,

Floats to me. In the enchainment
Of a travelling and a working wing
She comes shying, sidelong, settling
On the bare grave by the grain.

And I sleep, curled in my cold cave. . . .
Her wands quiver as a nostril quivers:
The gray veilings of the grave
Crumple, my limbs lock, reverse,

And work me, jointed, to the glance
That licks out to me in white fire
And, piercing, whirs *Remember*
Till my limbs catch. Life, life! I dance.

THE SPHINX'S RIDDLE
TO OEDIPUS

Not to have guessed is better: what is, ends,
But among fellows, with reluctance,
Clasped by the Woman-Breasted, Lion-Pawed.

To have clasped in one's own arms a mother,
To have killed with one's own hands a father
—Is not this, Lame One, to have been alone?

The seer is doomed for seeing; and to understand
Is to pluck out one's own eyes with one's own hands.
But speak: what has a woman's breasts, a lion's paws?

You stand at midday in the marketplace
Before your life: to see is to have spoken.
—Yet to see, Blind One, is to be alone.

JEROME

Each day brings its toad, each night its dragon.
Der heilige Hieronymus—his lion is at the zoo—
Listens, listens. All the long, soft, summer day
Dreams affright his couch, the deep boils like a pot.
As the sun sets, the last patient rises,
Says to him, *Father;* trembles, turns away.

Often, to the lion, the saint said, *Son.*
To the man the saint says—but the man is gone.
Under a plaque of Gradiva, at gloaming,
The old man boils an egg. When he has eaten
He listens a while. The patients have not stopped.
At midnight, he lies down where his patients lay.

All night the old man whispers to the night.
It listens evenly. The great armored paws
Of its forelegs put together in reflection,
It thinks: *Where Ego was, there Id shall be.*
The world wrestles with it and is changed into it
And after a long time changes it. The dragon

Listens as the old man says, at dawn: *I see*
—There is an old man, naked, in a desert, by a cliff.
He has set out his books, his hat, his ink, his shears
Among scorpions, toads, the wild beasts of the desert.
I lie beside him—I am a lion.
He kneels listening. He holds in his left hand

The stone with which he beats his breast, and holds
In his right hand, the pen with which he puts
Into his book, the words of the angel:
The angel up into whose face he looks.
But the angel does not speak. He looks into the face
Of the night, and the night says—but the night is gone.

He has slept. . . . At morning, when man's flesh is young
And man's soul thankful for it knows not what,
The air is washed, and smells of boiling coffee,
And the sun lights it. The old man walks placidly
To the grocer's; walks on, under leaves, in light,
To a lynx, a leopard—he has come:

The man holds out a lump of liver to the lion,
And the lion licks the man's hand with his tongue.

THE BRONZE DAVID
OF DONATELLO

A sword in his right hand, a stone in his left hand,
He is naked. Shod and naked. Hatted and naked.
The ribbons of his leaf-wreathed, bronze-brimmed bonnet
Are tasseled; crisped into the folds of frills,
Trills, graces, they lie in separation
Among the curls that lie in separation
Upon the shoulders.
                Lightly, as if accustomed,
Loosely, as if indifferent,
The boy holds in grace
The stone moulded, somehow, by the fingers,
The sword alien, somehow, to the hand.
                    The boy David
Said of it: "There is none like *that*."
                    The boy David's
Body shines in freshness, still unhandled,
And thrusts its belly out a little in exact
Shamelessness. Small, close, complacent,
A labyrinth the gaze retraces,
The rib-case, navel, nipples are the features
Of a face that holds us like the whore Medusa's—
Of a face that, like the genitals, is sexless.
What sex has victory?
The mouth's cut Cupid's-bow, the chin's unwinning dim-
   ple
Are tightened, a little oily, take, use, notice:
Centering itself upon itself, the sleek
Body with its too-large head, this green
Fruit now forever green, this offending

And efficient elegance draws subtly, supply,
Between the world and itself, a shining
Line of delimitation, demarcation.
The body mirrors itself.
                           Where the armpit becomes breast,
Becomes back, a great crow's-foot is slashed.
Yet who would gash
The sleek flesh so? the cast, filed, shining flesh?
The cuts are folds: these are the folds of flesh
That closes on itself as a knife closes.

The right foot is planted on a wing. Bent back in ease
Upon a supple knee—the toes curl a little, grasping
The crag upon which they are set in triumph—
The left leg glides toward, the left foot lies upon
A head. The head's other wing (the head is bearded
And winged and helmeted and bodiless)
Grows like a swan's wing up inside the leg;
Clothes, as the suit of a swan-maiden clothes,
The leg. The wing reaches, almost, to the rounded
Small childish buttocks. The dead wing warms the leg,
The dead wing, crushed beneath the foot, is swan's-
    down.
Pillowed upon the rock, Goliath's head
Lies under the foot of David.

Strong in defeat, in death rewarded,
The head dreams what has destroyed it
And is untouched by its destruction.
The stone sunk in the forehead, say the Scriptures;
There is no stone in the forehead. The head is helmed
Or else, unguarded, perfect still.
Borne high, borne long, borne in mastery,

The head is fallen.
                    The new light falls
As if in tenderness, upon the face—
Its masses shift for a moment, like an animal,
And settle, misshapen, into sleep: Goliath
Snores a little in satisfaction.

To so much strength, those overborne by it
Seemed girls, and death came to it like a girl,
Came to it, through the soft air, like a bird—
So that the boy is like a girl, is like a bird
Standing on something it has pecked to death.

The boy stands at ease, his hand upon his hip:
The truth of victory. A Victory
Angelic, almost, in indifference,
An angel sent with no message but this triumph
And alone, now, in his triumph,
He looks down at the head and does not see it.

Upon this head
As upon a spire, the boy David dances,
Dances, and is exalted.
                    Blessed are those brought low,
Blessed is defeat, sleep blessed, blessed death.

RANDALL JARRELL

was born in Nashville, Tennessee, in 1914 and gradu-
ated from Vanderbilt University. Mr. Jarrell taught at
Sarah Lawrence and Kenyon Colleges, the Universities
of Texas, Illinois, Indiana and Cincinnati, Princeton
University, and at the Woman's College of the University of North Carolina. At various times he was
poetry critic of *The Nation, Partisan Review* and *The
Yale Review,* and as poet, novelist and critic his work
received many awards. For two years he was Con-
sultant in Poetry at the Library of Congress. He was
a member of the National Institute of Arts and Letters
and a chancellor of The American Academy of Poets.
His books include seven volumes of poems, of which
the first four (*Blood for a Stranger, Little Friend,
Little Friend, Losses* and *The Seven-League Crutches*)
are included substantially complete in the *Selected
Poems;* the sixth is included as the second part of this
volume. His last book of poems, *The Lost World,* was
published in 1965. He was also the author of a work
of fiction (*Pictures from an Institution*), two volumes
of essays (*Poetry and the Age* and *A Sad Heart at the
Supermarket*), and three books for children (*The
Gingerbread Rabbit, The Bat Poet* and *The Animal
Family*). He died on October 14, 1965.

Atheneum Paperbacks

LITERATURE AND THE ARTS

Atheneum Paperbacks

POLITICAL SCIENCE

3